COMPANY
A MUSICAL COMEDY

TITLES BY STEPHEN SONDHEIM
ALSO AVAILABLE FROM TCG

Assassins, book by John Weidman

Gypsy, music by Jule Styne, book by Arthur Laurents

Into the Woods, book by James Lapine

Pacific Overtures, book by John Weidman

Passion, book by James Lapine

COMPANY
A MUSICAL COMEDY

MUSIC AND LYRICS BY

STEPHEN SONDHEIM

BOOK BY

GEORGE FURTH

THEATRE COMMUNICATIONS GROUP

1996

Company is published by Theatre Communications Group, Inc.,
355 Lexington Ave., New York, NY 10017-0217.

Sondheim, Stephen.
[Company. Libretto]
Company : a musical / music and lyrics by Stephen Sondheim ;
book by George Furth.
Libretto.
ISBN 1-55936-108-5
1. Musicals—Librettos. I. Furth, George, 1932—. II. Title.
ML50.S705C6 1995 <Case>
782. 1'4'0268—dc20
95-45985
CIP
MN

Book Design and Composition by Lisa Govan

First Printing, June 1996
Fourth Printing, November 2002

Company was originally presented by Harold Prince, in association with Ruth Mitchell, at the Alvin Theatre, New York, in April 1970. Sets and projections by Boris Aronson, costumes by D. D. Ryan, lighting by Robert Ornbo, orchestrations by Jonathan Tunick, musical direction by Harold Hastings, musical numbers staged by Michael Bennett, dance music arrangements by Wally Harper and direction by Harold Prince. The cast was as follows:

ROBERT	Dean Jones
SARAH	Barbara Barrie
HARRY	Charles Kimbrough
SUSAN	Merle Louise
PETER	John Cunningham
JENNY	Teri Ralston
DAVID	George Coe
AMY	Beth Howland
PAUL	Steve Elmore
JOANNE	Elaine Stritch
LARRY	Charles Braswell

MARTA	Pamela Myers
KATHY	Donna McKechnie
APRIL	Susan Browning
THE VOCAL	Cathy Corkill
MINORITY	Carol Gelfand
(unseen	Marilyn Saunders
chorus)	Dona D. Vaughn

Company opened at the Roundabout Theatre Company, New York City in October 1995. Sets by Tony Walton, projections by Wendall K. Harrington, costumes by William Ivey Long, lighting by Peter Kaczorowski, sound designed by Tony Meola, orchestrations by Jonathan Tunick, musical direction by David Loud, musical numbers staged by Rob Marshall, and direction by Scott Ellis. The cast was as follows:

ROBERT	Boyd Gaines
SARAH	Kate Burton
HARRY	Robert Westenberg
SUSAN	Patricia Ben Peterson
PETER	Jonathan Dokuchitz
JENNY	Diana Canova
DAVID	John Hillner
AMY	Veanne Cox
PAUL	Danny Burstein
JOANNE	Debra Monk
LARRY	Timothy Landfield

MARTA	La Chanze
KATHY	Charlotte D'Amboise
APRIL	Jane Krakowski

Company opened at the Donmar Warehouse, London in December 1995. Designed by Mark Thompson, lighting by Paul Pyant, sound designed by John A. Leonard, orchestrations by Jonathan Tunick, musical direction by Paddy Cunneen, musical numbers staged by Jonathan Butterell, and direction by Sam Mendes. The cast was as follows:

ROBERT	Adrian Lester
SARAH	Rebecca Front
HARRY	Clive Rowe
SUSAN	Clare Burt
PETER	Gareth Snook
JENNY	Liza Sadovy
DAVID	Teddy Kempner
AMY	Sophie Thompson
PAUL	Michael Simkins
JOANNE	Sheila Gish
LARRY	Paul Bentley
MARTA	Anna Francolini
KATHY	Kiran Hocking
APRIL	Hannah James

Musical Numbers

Act One

1.	Overture	*Orchestra*
2.	"Company"	*Robert and Company*
3.	"The Little Things You Do Together"	*Joanne and Couples*
4.	"Sorry-Grateful"	*Harry, David, Larry*
5.	"You Could Drive a Person Crazy"	*April, Kathy, Marta*
6.	"Have I Got a Girl for You"	*Husbands*
7.	"Someone Is Waiting"	*Robert*
8.	"Another Hundred People"	*Marta*
9.	"Getting Married Today"	*Amy, Paul, Susan or Jenny, and Company*
10.	"Marry Me a Little"	*Robert*

Act Two

1.	Entr'Acte	*Orchestra*
2.	"Side By Side By Side"/ "What Would We Do Without You"	*Robert and Couples*
3.	"Poor Baby"	*Wives*
4.	"Barcelona"	*Robert, April*
5.	"The Ladies Who Lunch"	*Joanne*
6.	"Being Alive"	*Robert*

This script is an amalgamation of the Roundabout
and Donmar Warehouse productions
of *Company*.

Song lyrics are indicated within the text by indenting the
lyrics one line below the character name.

Robert is the only member of the company who
doesn't double. The remaining thirteen members of the
company each have a particular character to play,
as well as doubling as Company.

There is no dancing or
singing ensemble.

ACT ONE

Scene One

Robert's empty apartment. Robert enters, crosses to the answering machine and hits the "play" button.

JOANNE *(Voice-over)*: Hi, this is a dirty phone call. Larry and I are going to be in the country so we'll miss any birthday celebrations. Anyway, you're thirty-five. Who wants to celebrate being that old? Well, I only hope I look as good as you when *I'm* your age.

(Sound of hang-up, followed by a buzz. A beep sound, then:)

PETER *(Voice-over)*: Hi, Bob. It's Peter. Get those girls out of your bed and pick up the phone, will ya? Oh, God, I am so envious I can't even talk. Call me.

(Sound of hang-up, followed by a buzz. A beep sound, then:)

APRIL *(Voice-over)*: Hi, Robert, it's April. *(Pause)* Oh. I forgot what I was going to say.

(Sound of hang-up, followed by a buzz. A beep sound, then:)

AMY *(Voice-over)*: Hi, Bobby, it's Amy. I just called to say that if I'm late for the party tonight please tell Paul that I'm running—oh, wait, you're not supposed to know that

3

there's a— *(Panic, as she tries to save herself)* Judy? Judy? Oh, goodness, I'm afraid I dialed a wrong number. Sorry. Just ignore this call. *(Speaking to someone else in the distance as she's hanging up)* Oh, God, you're never going to believe what I just did!

(Sound of hang-up, followed by a buzz. A beep sound, then:)

MARTA: Yo, Bob. It's Marta. Long time, no hear. Well, the doctor said false alarm, I'm not pregnant. So, hey, you can feel free to return my calls again, huh?

(Sound of hang-up, followed by a double beep, indicating the end of messages. Robert hits the "off" button, then sits and hits the "record" button and speaks into the machine)

ROBERT: Hi, this is Bob. Yes, today's my birthday. And yes, you may leave a message about how happy you are that I'm turning thirty-five. And whatever you're calling about my answer is yes.

(He hangs up; crosses to bar; pours a drink; crosses again; sits with his back to the audience; drinks; puts glass down and lowers his head in his hands a brief moment; his head comes up to a series of ghostly offstage individual voices intoning "Bobby" a capella; the voices increase in volume as the five married couples enter from various parts of the stage and group themselves around his apartment, facing the audience and him. They look out front and speak tonelessly. They carry wrapped presents)

My birthday. It's my birthday. Do you know you had me scared to death? I was just about to run out of this place like nobody's business. I was. I mean, I didn't know—I mean, what kind of friends would surprise you on your thirty-fifth birthday? *(Pause)* Mine. Then again, how many times do you get to be thirty-five? Eleven? *(Pause)* Okay, come on. Say it and get it over with. It's embarrassing. Quick. I can't stand it.

ALL BUT ROBERT *(Intoning)*: Happy birthday, Robert.

ROBERT: I stood it. Thank you for including me in your thoughts, your lives, your families. Yes, thank you for remembering. Thank you.

ALL BUT ROBERT *(Intoning)*: You don't look it.

ROBERT: Well, I feel it.

ALL BUT ROBERT *(Intoning)*: It's the birthday boy!

ROBERT: Now you've rehearsed. Very good. I am touched.

SUSAN *(Intoning)*: I love it when people are really surprised.

PETER *(Intoning)*: She loves it when people are really surprised.

SARAH *(Intoning)*: If you don't like it, you can take it back.

ROBERT: Well, I haven't even seen it yet.

SARAH *(Intoning)*: I mean, though, if you don't like it—

HARRY *(Intoning)*: Why don't you wait until the man looks at the thing?

ROBERT: I know I'll like it.

SARAH *(Intoning)*: Why don't you just take it back?

(Gradually, they all start becoming more human, looking and reacting to Robert and to each other)

HARRY: For God's sake, he just said he likes it.

SARAH: Pretend not to notice Harry, Robert. I think I'll leave.

HARRY: I was being funny, Sarah. We could stay a little longer.

PETER *(Throwing present)*: Hey, Bobby, take ours back too.

AMY *(Bringing hers to Robert)*: Here's from Paul and me. If I were you, I would take it back and get the money. It cost so much I fainted.

PAUL: It did not, Robert. It's a sweater.

AMY: You told him what it was! *(To Robert)* Well, when I saw the price tag, I thought it was a house.

JOANNE *(As Jenny starts toward Robert)*: Miss, Miss. YOU! Yes, you! Tell him to take yours back and get the money. It's not the gift, it's the cost that counts.

JENNY *(Handing her present to Robert)*: Who *is* that?

JOANNE: That is I, Miss. I am very rich and *(Indicating Larry)* I am married to him, and I'd introduce him, but I forgot his name.

LARRY: Many happy returns of the day, old man.

JENNY: David is now going to deliver our greeting. Go on, sweetheart.

DAVID: Robert. Happy birthday from us.

ALL BUT ROBERT: Happy birthday!

PETER: And may this year bring you fame, fortune and your first wife.

ALL BUT ROBERT: Here, here.

ROBERT: Listen, I'm fine without the three.

JOANNE: You bet your ass, baby.

SUSAN *(To Joanne)*: He might have meant that superciliously.

JOANNE *(A look to Susan)*: Oooo, isn't she darling with all that free help.

LARRY *(Referring to Joanne)*: She's a great kidder.

(Joanne laughs hugely, throwing a kiss to Susan)

See what I mean?

ROBERT: All right. Let's cut out the many happy returns and that is about enough about me. I am just indeed lucky to have all of you. I mean, when you've got friends like mine . . .

(Amy enters with a cake and begins to sing "Happy Birthday." The group joins in. They finish the song and then they speak, call, applaud:)

ALL BUT ROBERT: Yeah! Hooray! *(Etc.)*

AMY: Blow out your candles and make a wish.

JENNY: Don't tell your wish, Bobby, or it won't come true.

SUSAN: You have to close your eyes and blow them all out.

SARAH: Be sure you make it a good one, Robert.

(Robert closes his eyes, wishes, blows, but the candles stay lit. He tries again. He fails again. Amy exits with the cake and returns. As the following lines are spoken, each couple begins to exit. By the time the singing starts, Robert is alone, his friends watching him from a distance. Music begins)

JENNY: You still get your wish. He still gets his wish.

SUSAN: He does? It must be a new rule!

SARAH: Sure you do.

JOANNE: Don't believe a word of it.

AMY: Of course you do.

ROBERT: Oh, I know it. I will. Actually, I didn't wish for anything.

LARRY: He's kidding. You gotta be kidding.

DAVID: Anyway, don't tell it.

PETER: Tell it if it's dirty.

PAUL: They say you're not supposed to tell it.

AMY: Paul's right. Don't tell.

HARRY: Anyway, Robert, you're in your prime—thirty-five.

SARAH: Harry, hush! You don't tell a person's age at our ages.

JENNY:

Bobby . . .

PETER:

    Bobby . . .

AMY:

    Bobby baby . . .

PAUL:

    Bobby bubi . . .

JOANNE:

    Robby . . .

SUSAN:

    Robert darling . . .

DAVID:

    Bobby, we've been trying to call you.

JENNY:

    Bobby . . .

LARRY:

    Bobby . . .

AMY:

    Bobby baby . . .

PAUL:

    Bobby bubi . . .

SARAH:

    Angel, I've got something to tell you.

HARRY:

    Bob . . .

LARRY:

Rob-o . . .

JOANNE:

Bobby, love . . .

SUSAN:

Bobby, honey . . .

AMY & PAUL:

Bobby, we've been trying to reach you all day.

LARRY:

Bobby . . .

HARRY:

Bobby . . .

PETER:

Bobby baby . . .

SARAH:

Angel . . .

JOANNE:

Darling . . .

DAVID & JENNY:

The kids were asking, Bobby . . .

HARRY:

Bobby . . .

SUSAN:

Robert . . .

JOANNE:

Robby . . .

PETER:

Bob-o . . .

LARRY & JOANNE:

Bobby, there was something we wanted to say.

SARAH & HARRY:

Bobby . . .

PAUL:

Bobby bubi . . .

AMY:

Sweetheart . . .

SUSAN:

Sugar . . .

DAVID & JENNY:

Your line was busy.

PETER:

What have you been up to, kiddo?

AMY & PAUL:

Bobby, Bobby, how have you been?

HARRY:

Fella . . .

SARAH:

Sweetie,

HARRY & SARAH:
> How have you been?

PETER & susan:
> Bobby, Bobby, how have you been?

DAVID, JENNY, JOANNE & LARRY:
> Stop by on your way home—

AMY & PAUL:
> Seems like weeks since we talked to you!

HARRY & SARAH:
> Bobby, we've been thinking of you!

PETER & SUSAN:
> Bobby, we've been thinking of you!

DAVID, JENNY, JOANNE & LARRY:
> Drop by any time!

AMY & PAUL:
> Bobby, there's a concert on Tuesday.

DAVID & JENNY:
> Hank and Mary get into town tomorrow.

PETER & SUSAN:
> How about some Scrabble on Sunday?

SARAH & HARRY:
> Why don't we all go to the beach—

JOANNE & LARRY:
> Bob, we're having people in Saturday night.

HARRY & SARAH:
>Next weekend?

JENNY:
>Bobby . . .

PETER:
>Bobby . . .

AMY:
>Bobby, baby . . .

DAVID & JENNY:
>Whatcha doing Thursday?

HARRY:
>Bobby . . .

SARAH:
>Angel . . .

PAUL:
>Bobby bubi . . .

SARAH & HARRY:
>Time we got together, is Wednesday all right?

AMY:
>Bobby . . .

LARRY:
>Rob-o . . .

SUSAN:
>Bobby, honey . . .

AMY & PAUL:
> Eight o'clock on Monday.

JOANNE:
> Robby, darling . . .

PETER:
> Bobby fella . . .

PETER & JOANNE:
> Bobby baby . . .

ALL BUT ROBERT:
> Bobby, come on over for dinner!
> We'll be so glad to see you!
> Bobby, come on over for dinner!
> Just be the three of us,
> Only the three of us!
> We looooove you!

ROBERT:
> Phone rings, door chimes, in comes company!
> No strings, good times, room hums, company!
> Late nights, quick bites, party games,
> Deep talks, long walks, telephone calls,
> Thoughts shared, souls bared, private names,
> All those photos up on the walls
> "With love,"
> With love filling the days,
> With love seventy ways,
> "To Bobby with love"
> From all
> Those
> Good and crazy people, my friends,

Those
Good and crazy people, my married friends!
And that's what it's all about, isn't it?

ALL BUT ROBERT:
That's what it's really about,
Really about!

(Kathy, Marta and April enter)

APRIL:
Bobby . . .

KATHY:
Bobby . . .

MARTA:
Bobby baby . . .

PAUL:
Bobby bubi . . .

JOANNE:
Robby . . .

SUSAN:
Robert darling

SARAH:
Angel, will you do me a favor?

LARRY:
Bobby . . .

AMY:

> Bobby . . .

ROBERT:

> Name it, Sarah.

JENNY:

> Bobby baby . . .

PAUL:

> Bobby bubi . . .

PETER:

> Listen pal, I'd like your opinion . . .

HARRY:

> Bob . . .

LARRY:

> Rob-o . . .

ROBERT:

> Try me, Peter . . .

KATHY:

> Bobby love . . .

MARTA:

> Bobby honey . . .

LARRY & AMY:

> Bobby, there's a problem, I need your advice . . .

APRIL & PAUL:

> Bobby . . .

MARTA & HARRY:

> Bobby . . .

KATHY & PETER:

> Bobby baby . . .

SARAH:

> Angel . . .

JOANNE:

> Darling . . .

APRIL, MARTA & KATHY:

> Just half an hour . . .

ROBERT:

> Amy, can I call you tomorrow?

DAVID & JENNY:

> Honey, if you'd visit the kids once or twice . . .

SARAH & PETER:

> Bobby . . .

JOANNE & HARRY:

> Bobby . . .

PAUL & MARTA:

> Bobby bubi . . .

AMY:

> Sweetheart . . .

SUSAN:

> Sugar . . .

APRIL, MARTA & KATHY:
> What's happened to you?

ROBERT:
> Jenny, I could take them to the zoo on Friday.

WIVES:
> Bobby . . . Bobby . . . where have you been?

HUSBANDS:
> Fella . . . kiddo . . . where have you been?

APRIL, MARTA & KATHY:
> Bobby . . . Bobby . . . how have you been?

HARRY, SARAH, PETER & SUSAN:
> Stop by on your way home . . .

ROBERT:
> Susan, love, I'll make it after seven
> If I can.

WIVES:
> Bobby, dear, I don't mean to pry . . .

HUSBANDS:
> Bobby, we've been thinking of you!

APRIL, MARTA & KATHY:
> Bobby, we've been thinking of you!

PAUL, AMY, JOANNE, LARRY, DAVID & JENNY:
> Drop by any time . . .

ROBERT:
>Sorry, Paul, I made a date with Larry and Joanne.

WIVES:
>Bobby dear, it's none of my business . . .

HUSBANDS:
>Lookit, pal, I have to work Thursday evening . . .

WIVES:
>Darling, you've been looking peculiar . . .

HUSBANDS:
>Bobby boy, you know how I hate the opera . . .

WIVES:
>Funny thing, your name came up only last night.

ROBERT:
>Harry . . . David . . . Kathy, I . . .

APRIL, MARTA & KATHY:
>I shouldn't say this but . . .

ROBERT:
>April . . . Marta . . . Listen, people . . .

WIVES:
>Bobby, we've been worried, you sure you're all right?

HUSBANDS:
>Bobby . . . Bobby . . . Bobby baby . . .

APRIL, MARTA & KATHY:
>Did I do something wrong?

HUSBANDS:
> Bobby bubi, Bobby fella, Bobby, Bobby . . .

COMPANY:
> Bobby, come on over for dinner!
> We'll be so glad to see you!
> Bobby, come on over for dinner!
> Just be the three of us,
> Only the three of us,
> We looooooooooooove you!

> Phone rings, door chimes, in comes company!
> No strings, good times, just chums, company!
> Late nights, quick bites, party games,
> Deep talks, long walks, telephone calls,
> Thoughts shared, souls bared, private names,
> All those photos up on the walls
> "With love,"
> With love filling the days,
> With love seventy ways,
> "To Bobby, with love"
> From all
> Those
> Good and crazy people, my friends,
> Those good and crazy people, my married friends!
> And that's what it's all about, isn't it?
> That's what it's really about, isn't it?
> That's what it's really about, really about?

HUSBANDS:
> Isn't it? Isn't it? Isn't it? Isn't it?

WIVES, APRIL, MARTA & KATHY:
> Love . . .

HUSBANDS:

    Isn't it? Isn't it? Isn't it? Isn't it?

ROBERT:

    You I love and you I love and you and you I
    Love
    And you I love and you I love and you and
    You I love, I love you!

ALL:

    Company! Company! Company,
    Lots of company!
    Life is company!
    Love is company!
    Company!

(A montage of city sounds is heard as the following lines are spoken on the Company's exit; these lines are spoken quickly, overlapping each other)

SARAH: Harry, it's the door. I'll get it.

HARRY: I've got it.

SARAH: *I'll* get it. I always do.

JOANNE: What was that clock chime?

LARRY: Five o'clock.

JOANNE: Thank God, cocktail hour!

APRIL: Final departure call for NSEW Airlines flight 119. Will the passengers that have not boarded please do so.

PETER: What the hell is that noise?

SUSAN: They're either cleaning the building next door or tearing it down.

KATHY: Taxi! Taxi! Oh, please, please!

MARTA: Will you stop blowing that horn, you yo-yo!

AMY: Paul, what is that noise?

PAUL: I don't hear anything.

JENNY: Oh, David, the phone.

DAVID: I'm getting it.

JENNY: Oh, the kids. It's gonna wake up the kids.

Scene Two

Sarah and Harry's living room on the ground floor of a garden apartment. Sarah, Harry and Robert have finished a long dinner and are having coffee in the living room.

SARAH *(Pouring coffee)*: There's cinnamon in the coffee, Robert . . . the odd taste is cinnamon. Sugar and cream?

ROBERT: Both. May I have lots of both?

SARAH: Of course you may.

HARRY: Do you want some brandy in it, Robert?

ROBERT: You having some?

SARAH: We don't drink, but you have some, you darling. Go ahead.

HARRY: Or do you want a real drink? We have anything you want.

ROBERT: Well, Harry, if you don't mind, could I have some bourbon?

HARRY: Right.

SARAH: Sweetheart!

HARRY: Okay, darling.

ROBERT *(As Harry gets the bourbon)*: Are you both on the wagon? Sarah? You're not on the wagon?

SARAH: Goodness, Robert, all the questions! Or do you just collect trivia like some old quiz show contestant? We spend half of our lives with you and now you notice Harry's on the wagon?

HARRY: A year and a half.

SARAH: No, love. Just a year.

HARRY: It was a year in February. It's a year and a half now.

SARAH: I know for a fact next month it will be a year.

HARRY: And a half.

SARAH: One year. Count it, one! Harry got arrested for being drunk and quit out of some kind of humiliation.

HARRY: I quit to see if I could is actually what happened. C'mon, I must have told you about all that.

ROBERT: Never. You never mentioned it or I never would have brought the bourbon. How were you arrested?

SARAH: Another question! Here, why don't you have one of these brownies you brought?

HARRY: I was in California on business and I really got soused one night and these guys drove me back to my hotel but instead of going in, I walked down to the corner to get something to eat to sober up.

SARAH: You said it was three blocks.

HARRY: No, just the corner.

SARAH *(Stage whisper to Robert)*: Three blocks.

HARRY: Anyway, this patrol car stopped me and said, "You're drunk." I said, "Drunk? I'm clobbered." He said, "I'm taking you in." "Take me to my hotel, for God's sake," I said, "it's just on the corner."

SARAH: Three blocks away.

HARRY: Anyway, they mugged me and booked me for being drunk. Unbelievable. And then, Robert, the very next time I was out there, I got arrested all over again—drunk driving. I only had wine—

SARAH: Only three bottles . . .

HARRY: And I *insisted* on taking a drunk test. I flunked it by one point.

SARAH: And that is when you quit, precious. He always thinks it was the first arrest, but it was the second. We never told you that? Curious, I thought Harry had told *everybody*.

HARRY: Anyway, I quit to see if I really had a drinking problem, and I don't.

SARAH: Just a problem drinking.

ROBERT: Do you miss it?

SARAH: See how you talk in questions! Harry, do you miss it?

HARRY: No. No, I really don't.

SARAH: Yes. Yes, he really does. Hi, darling.

HARRY: Anyway, I stopped, haven't had a drink since.

SARAH: Whoops.

HARRY: What's whoops? I haven't had a drink since.

SARAH *(Singing)*: At Sheila and George's wedding.

HARRY: A toast, for God's sake. Sorry, Robert, you must have noticed how staggering falling-down drunk I got on one swallow of Champagne.

SARAH: I never said you got drunk, but you did have the Champagne.

HARRY: A swallow. One swallow.

SARAH: And it was gone. An elephant swallow.

ROBERT: I'd like to ask for another bourbon, but I'm terrified.

SARAH: Darling Robert, put a nipple on the bottle for all we care. Don't you want a brownie?

ROBERT: God, no. I'll bust.

SARAH: Bust? You bust! You skinny thing. Just look at you. Bones. You're skin and bones. I bet when you get on a scale it goes the other way—minus.

ROBERT: Well, thank you, Sarah. I am touched and honored. And I think I was just insulted.

SARAH: Oh, Robert, I was praying that you'd eat just one so I could watch.

ROBERT: Sarah! Is it possible you've become a food voyeur?

SARAH: Mexican food. What I crave without cease is Mexican food. With all the Tabasco sauce in the world.

HARRY: Don't eat that brownie!

SARAH: I'm not. I'm just smelling it. Oh, Robert, you eat one!

ROBERT: Not with bourbon.

SARAH: And chocolate. I'd kill for chocolate. Or a baked potato with sour cream and chives. Doesn't that just make you writhe? Or hot sourdough bread and all the butter there is.

HARRY: Chili.

SARAH: Oh, chili, dear God, yes, chili!

HARRY: Manicotti.

SARAH: Manicotti. One teaspoon of manicotti.

HARRY: Sara Lee cake.

SARAH: Sara Lee cake! Sara Lee is the most phenomenal woman since Eleanor Roosevelt.

HARRY: How about sweet and sour shrimp?

SARAH: How about sweet and sour anything?

(Sarah pretends to pass out, and sticks a brownie in her mouth as she slides under the table. She eats it, thinking she is hidden from sight. As Robert watches her, Harry downs Robert's bourbon. Then both Sarah and Harry casually turn, their attention now back on Robert)

ROBERT: I get the impression you guys are on diets.

HARRY: Not me, Sarah.

SARAH: Look at these pants. You can put your fist in there. That's how much weight I've lost.

HARRY: She always does that. Look, I can put my fist in my pants too, you know. She thinks I buy that.

SARAH: Darling, I've lost eight pounds already.

HARRY: It's the magazines, Robert. Did you ever look at any of those women's magazines? Pages and pages of cakes and pies and roasts and potatoes. I bet Sarah subscribes to about forty magazines. It's a sickness. We're up to our ass in magazines.

SARAH: I read them all.

HARRY: Don't.

SARAH: Do.

HARRY: Look at this, Robert. Wrestling. She even subscribes to a magazine on wrestling.

SARAH: Karate, not wrestling. It's karate.

HARRY: Wouldn't you like to see it? All those fat broads in her gym learning karate. What wouldn't you give to see that?

SARAH: Strangely enough, darling, I'm terribly good at it.

ROBERT: How long have you been studying it?

SARAH: Who asked that question? Oh, Robert! Seven months.

HARRY: Show us some karate.

SARAH: No. Robert, would you like some more coffee, love? You, Harry?

HARRY: No. I want some karate. I want to see how my money is being wasted.

SARAH: No.

ROBERT: Do one thing.

SARAH: No.

ROBERT: Come on, Sarah, I really would give anything to see you do just one. I bet you are excellent. Hey, I'll be your partner.

SARAH: No. Oh, Harry, this is embarrassing.

HARRY: Aw, come on.

SARAH: My God—all right.

HARRY: Hooray!

SARAH: One throw!

HARRY: Hooray!

SARAH: Harry, do you want to stand there?

HARRY: Where?

SARAH: There.

HARRY: All right. I'm standing here. Now what?

(Sarah goes into her karate preparation ritual)

SARAH: Okay. Now just come at me.
HARRY: Okay.

(Harry goes at her and she lets out a piercing samurai sound, flipping him to the floor)

ROBERT: Fantastic. That's hysterical.
HARRY: Actually, I could have prevented that.
SARAH: How?
HARRY: By blocking it.
SARAH: No, that can't be blocked.
HARRY: It certainly can. I just didn't do it.
SARAH: Anyway, Robert, that can't be blocked.
HARRY: Let's do it again.
SARAH: All right, darling.
HARRY: I'll come at you again.
SARAH: Okay.

(He goes at her. She attempts the same thing and he blocks it)

Oh, I see. Put me down. Okay, do it again.

(He does it again and she overcomes his block, throwing him again. She then screams and jumps on top of him, holding him down. Joanne appears and looks at them for a moment)

JOANNE:
      It's the little things you do together,
      Do together,
      Do together,
      That make perfect relationships.
      The hobbies you pursue together,
      Savings you accrue together,
      Looks you misconstrue together

That make marriage a joy.
Mm-hm . . .

ROBERT: That's very good.
HARRY: Once more. Do it once more.
ROBERT: Harry, could I have another bourbon?

(Harry lunges at Sarah. They block each other and are caught in a power struggle)

HARRY: Give up?
SARAH: Do you?
HARRY: I've got you.
SARAH: I've got *you.*
HARRY: Do you want to do it again?
SARAH: All right. You break first.
HARRY: Uh-uh. You break first.
SARAH: We can just stay here.
HARRY: All right with me. Fine with me.
ROBERT: You're both very good.
BOTH: Thank you.
HARRY: I could get out of this, you know.
SARAH: Try it.

(Harry kicks a foot behind Sarah's feet, knocking her to the floor. Then he gets on top of her, pinning her down)

HARRY: Okay, I tried it.

(Sarah pulls Harry by his shirt over her head, somersaulting aside, and to the floor. She gets up, grabs his arm, and, with her foot in his armpit, pins him down)

SARAH: Uncle?

HARRY: Uncle, your ass!

JOANNE:

It's the little things you share together,
Swear together,
Wear together,
That make perfect relationships.

The concerts you enjoy together,
Neighbors you annoy together,
Children you destroy together,
That keep marriage intact.

It's not so hard to be married
When two maneuver as one.
It's not so hard to be married
And, Jesus Christ, is it fun.

It's sharing little winks together,
Drinks together,
Kinks together,
That makes marriage a joy.

It's bargains that you shop together,
Cigarettes you stop together,
Clothing that you swap together
That make perfect relationships.

Uh-huh . . .
Mm-hm . . .

(Sarah and Harry break and prepare for a third fall)

ROBERT: Could I have another bourbon?

(Robert is hit from the front and rear by Harry and Sarah. All three go to the floor. The couples enter and sing with Joanne)

GROUP:

It's not talk of God and the decade ahead that
Allows you to get through the worst.
It's "I do" and "You don't" and "Nobody said that"
And "Who brought the subject up first?"
It's the little things, the little things, the
Little things . . .
It's the little things, the little things, the
Little things . . .

JENNY, DAVID, AMY & PAUL:

The little ways you try together,

SUSAN, PETER, JOANNE & LARRY:

Cry together,

JENNY, DAVID, AMY & PAUL:

Lie together

GROUP:

That make perfect relationships,

SUSAN, PETER, JOANNE & LARRY:

Becoming a cliche together,

JENNY, DAVID, AMY & PAUL:

Growing old and gray together,

JOANNE:

Withering away together

29

GROUP:

> That makes marriage a joy.

MEN & JOANNE:

> It's not so hard to be married,

WOMEN:

> It's much the cleanest of crimes.

MEN & JOANNE:

> It's not so hard to be married,

JOANNE:

> I've done it three or four times.

JENNY:

> It's people that you hate together,

PAUL & AMY:

> Bait together,

PETER & SUSAN:

> Date together,

GROUP:

> That make marriage a joy.

DAVID:

> It's things like using force together,

LARRY:

> Shouting till you're hoarse together,

JOANNE:

> Getting a divorce together,

GROUP:

> That make perfect relationships.

> Uh-huh . . .
> Kiss, kiss . . .

JOANNE:

> Mm-hm.

> *(Joanne and the couples exit. Robert, Sarah and Harry break)*

ROBERT: Why . . . wow . . . how 'bout that? Huh?

HARRY: I had you there . . .

SARAH: I had *you* there . . .

> *(They start for each other again, but Robert steps between them)*

ROBERT: I'd say it was a draw. Wow. Look at the time. I've got to get going.

SARAH & HARRY: Awwww!

ROBERT: Wow. Listen, I had a great time.

SARAH: So did we.

HARRY: Great to see you. Sure you wouldn't care for a night-cap?

ROBERT: Right!

> *(As Harry turns to get him a drink; stopping him)*

> I mean, no! I mean, will I see you guys soon?

SARAH: Don't answer that, Harry. He gets no more questions, that sneaky Pete.

(Robert turns to exit, stops)

ROBERT *(To himself)*: Wow.

(Underscoring: "Bobby Baby" music. Robert turns back to Sarah and Harry)

Thanks again.

(Sarah and Harry wave as Robert begins to leave slowly, utterly bewildered. Harry heads for the bar as Sarah pops a brownie in her mouth. Before making a full exit, Robert stops. He observes the following moment between Sarah and Harry)

HARRY: I'll turn out the lights.
SARAH *(With mouth very full)*: I will! I always do.
HARRY: No, you don't.
SARAH: Oh, Harry, I love you.

(She exits. Harry steals a drink)

ROBERT: Harry? You ever sorry you got married?

HARRY:

> You're always sorry,
> You're always grateful,
> You're always wondering what might have been.
> Then she walks in.
>
> And still you're sorry,
> And still you're grateful,
> And still you wonder and still you doubt,
> And she goes out.

> Everything's different,
> Nothing's changed,
> Only maybe slightly
> Rearranged.
>
> You're sorry-grateful,
> Regretful-happy,
> Why look for answers where none occur?
> You always are what you always were,
> Which has nothing to do with,
> All to do with her.

SARAH *(Offstage)*: Harry, darling, come to bed.
HARRY: Coming, darling.

(He stands still. The lights go down. Robert listens as David appears and sings)

DAVID:

> You're always sorry,
> You're always grateful,
> You hold her thinking, "I'm not alone."
> You're still alone.
>
> You don't live for her,
> You do live with her,
> You're scared she's starting to drift away
> And scared she'll stay.

(Larry enters)

LARRY:

> Good things get better,
> Bad get worse.
> Wait—I think I meant that in reverse.

HARRY, LARRY & DAVID:

  ·   You're sorry-grateful,
Regretful-happy,
Why look for answers where none occur?
You'll always be what you always were,
Which has nothing to do with, all to do with her.

(David exits)

HARRY & LARRY:

You'll always be what you always were,
Which has nothing to do with, all to do with her.

(Larry exits)

HARRY:

Nothing to do with,
All to do with her.

(Lights fade)

Scene Three

Peter and Susan's terrace. Robert stands alone.

PETER *(Offstage)*: Bob? Bob? Where the hell are you?

ROBERT: Out here.

PETER *(Entering, with Susan)*: For crissake, what are you doing
out here?

ROBERT: Oh, it is so great to have a terrace in this city. Wow.

SUSAN: Really? We just use it to store old sleds and stuff.

PETER *(Indicating)*: Look. Hundreds of thousand of terraces
in New York and never have I seen a single person out
on even one of them.

SUSAN: Plus you worry about kids tracking in dirt or falling over.

PETER: And everyone can hear everything you say. *(Leans over, calls up)* Are you listening? *(To Susan and Robert)* Not to mention look at all the bird-doo.

(Robert quickly removes his jacket from the railing)

SUSAN: And noisy?!! You cannot even hear yourself think. And what can you see? All you can see is the building across the street.

PETER *(Leaning over)*: Well, if you lean way out and look over there you can see the East River.

SUSAN *(Pulling Peter back)*: Except that you really can't. Peter almost met his Maker one night trying to see that dumb ol' East River. He did.

ROBERT: You saved him?

SUSAN: Me? No. Well, I suppose, in a way.

PETER: She fainted so I got down.

SUSAN: Peter just is not afraid of anything at all. Unfortunately, I simply was not made that way. One day Peter fell off the ladder when he was putting up my curio cabinet and he split his head right open. Well, I fainted. I came to, I looked at his head and I fainted again.

PETER: Four times she fainted that night.

ROBERT *(Laughing)*: Well, see now, to me that is so sweet. That is charm. Oh, you gotta be one lucky guy, Peter. I mean, hey, that kind of—Southern graciousness—there just ain't much of that around these parts. You two are—he said with envy—just beautiful together. Really a terrific pair. And Peter—if you ever decide to leave her—I want to be the first to know.

SUSAN *(Smiling at Peter)*: Well . . .

PETER: You're the first to know.

SUSAN *(Elated)*: We're getting divorced.
PETER: We haven't told anyone yet.
ROBERT *(Stunned)*: Oh.

(Underscoring: "Bobby Baby" music)

I'm—uh, so surprised.

(Susan and Peter stand smiling, just looking at Robert)

Maybe you'll work it out.

(The underscoring continues as Susan and Peter smile blankly)

Don't think so, huh? *(To Peter)* Well, I'm sure nobody can imagine how you feel. *(To Susan)* Or *you* feel. *(Turning; to himself, as he begins to exit)* Or *I* feel.

(Lights fade on the terrace as Robert exits)

Scene Four

Jenny and David's den. Jenny, Robert and David sit staring out front. A couple of toys are scattered around.

JENNY *(Rapidly, answering Robert's line from the previous scene)*:
Feel? I just don't feel anything. Here, David, I don't care for any more. It's too small. That's too small. It probably just doesn't work on me. Do you feel anything, David? Do you, honey? Because I don't.
ROBERT: You will.
JENNY: *When!* I mean, we've had *two* for heaven's sake. I think maybe it depends on the person's constitution. Don't

you, Dave? Well, listen, it's always good to try everything once.

ROBERT: Just wait!

JENNY: I'm not planning to go anywhere. Maybe I'm just too
dumb or square, but I honestly don't feel anything. Do
you, Dave? Because I don't. Absolutely nothing. Honestly,
not a thing. I mean, I *wish* I did. I just don't. Maybe they
gave you *real* grass, right off the front lawn. I knew I
wouldn't feel anything, though. I don't have that kind of
constitution. Why am I talking so much?

ROBERT: You're stoned.

JENNY: Am I? Am I? I am not.

DAVID: I am.

JENNY: Are you? You are not. I'm so dry!

ROBERT: You're stoned.

JENNY: Is that part of it?

ROBERT: You'll probably get hungry too.

JENNY: Yes? Should I feel *that*, too?

ROBERT: You don't have to feel anything.

JENNY: Are you hungry, Dave?

DAVID: No. I'd like some water, though.

JENNY: Me, too. Do you want some, Robert?

ROBERT: No, thank you.

JENNY: What?

ROBERT: I already have some, Jenny, thank you.

JENNY: Some what Robert?

DAVID: You asked him, honey. Water!

JENNY: Oh, water . . . I could not remember what we were talking about.

ROBERT: See, you forget when you're high!

JENNY: Ohhhh. God, do you. Wow. Are you high, Dave?

DAVID: I'm potted.

JENNY: Potted. That is beautiful. Jesus!

ROBERT: You're really high now, huh?

JENNY: Jesus!

DAVID: That's twice you said "Jesus."

JENNY: You're kidding.

DAVID: No. You said it two times. She never swears.

JENNY: I didn't even know I said it once.

DAVID: Say "son of a bitch."

JENNY: Son of a bitch.

(They all laugh)

DAVID: Say "Kiss my ass."

JENNY: Kiss my ass.

(They roar at this)

Kiss my ass, you son of a bitch.

(They scream with laughter)

Oh, Jesus. That's three!

(They laugh)

Shhh. Shhh. You'll wake the kids. Let's laugh to ourselves.

DAVID: Oh Jenny, for God's sake.

(Robert laughs more and pounds the floor)

JENNY: Sshh! We'll get evicted!

ROBERT: Jenny, you're terrific. You're the girl I should have married.

JENNY: Listen, I know a darling girl in this building you'll just love.

ROBERT: What?

JENNY: When are you going to get married?

DAVID: What?

JENNY: I mean it. To me a person's not complete until he's married.

DAVID: He's complete enough. *(To Robert)* You're better off the way you are.

ROBERT: That's what I hear.

JENNY *(Almost hurt)*: Oh, Dave. Do you mean that?

DAVID: No. *(Pause)* Well, frankly, sometimes I'd like to be single.

JENNY *(Now she is hurt)*: Oh. That's not even funny.

DAVID: It has nothing to do with you.

JENNY: I'm your wife!

DAVID: And that's the way I want it. But didn't you ever wish you could be single again? I mean for an hour even?

JENNY: No. *(Pause)* Could you make it two hours?

(She and Robert laugh)

Now Bobby, you get yourself married. You see the ideas you're giving Dave.

ROBERT: Oh, I will. It's not like I'm avoiding marriage. It's avoiding me, if anything. I'm ready.

JENNY: Actually, you're not. But listen, not everybody should be married, I guess.

DAVID: I don't know. Actually a man should be married. Your life has a—what? What am I trying to say? A point to it—a bottom. You know what I'm saying? I have every-thing—but freedom. Which is everything, huh? No. This is everything. I got my wife, my kids, a home. I feel that—uh—well, you gotta give up to get. Know what I'm saying?

ROBERT: Listen, I agree. But you know what bothers me is, if you marry, then you've got another person there all the time. Plus you can't get out of it whenever you just might want to get out of it. You are caught! See? And even if you do get out of it, what do you have to show for it? Not to mention the fact that—then—you've always been married. I mean, you can never not have been married again.

JENNY: I don't feel you're really ready. Do you think, just maybe I mean subconsciously—you might be resisting it?

ROBERT: No. Negative. Absolutely not! I have no block, no resistance. I am ready to be married.

JENNY *(Quietly)*: Then why aren't you?

(Pause)

ROBERT: I've always had things to accomplish. That's the main reason. First I had to finish school. Then I wanted to get started, to get some kind of security. And, uh—just things I wanted to do before I could even begin to think in terms of marriage. Oh, I know that can sound like rationalization, but it's not. Frankly, I wanted to have some fun before I settled down.

(Slight pause)

DAVID: Right. And you've done all those things.

ROBERT: Right. *(Pause)* Then why am I not married, huh? Wow. Taking me on a bummer. Wait though. You just wait. You are going to see major changes in my life. I mean I meet women all the time. All over the place. All you have to do is live in New York and you meet a girl a minute. And I've met some real special ladies recently. Like right now, I'm dating this flight attendant. Cute, original . . .

(April appears as we hear underscoring of "Bobby Baby" music)

... odd. And Kathy, you guys never met Kathy, did you? Well, she's the best ...

(Kathy appears)

... I'm talking the best! And then there's Marta.

(Marta appears)

God, now she is fun! I'm certainly not resisting marriage!

(Kathy, Marta and April react to this)

I mean it when I say my life is totally prepared for a gigantic change right now. I am ready to be married.

DAVID: Right. Then why aren't you?

ROBERT: Right!

APRIL: Right.

KATHY: Right.

MARTA: Right.

KATHY, MARTA & APRIL:
> Doo-doo-doo-doo
> Doo-doo-doo-doo
> Doo-doo-doo-doo-doo-doo.
> You could drive a person crazy,
> You could drive a person mad.
> Doo-doo doo-doo doo.
> First you make a person hazy
> So a person could be had.
> Doo-doo doo-doo-doo.

Then you leave a person dangling sadly
Outside your door,
Which it only makes a person gladly
Want you even more.

I could understand a person
If he said to go away.
Doo-doo doo-doo doo.
I could understand a person
If he happened to be gay.
Doo-doo doo-doo doo
Boo-boo-boo-boo.

But worse'n that,
A person that
Titillates a person and then leaves her flat
Is crazy,
He's a troubled person,
He's a truly crazy person
Himself!

(The women ad lib: "You turkey, jerk, idiot, monster, creep, loser, son of a bitch, cretin," etc.)

KATHY:

When a person's personality is personable,
He shouldn't oughta sit like a lump.
It's harder than a matador coercin' a bull
To try to get you off of your rump.
So single and attentive and attractive a man
Is everything a person could wish,
But turning off a person is the act of a man
Who likes to pull the hooks out of fish.

KATHY, MARTA & APRIL:

Knock, knock, is anybody there?
Knock, knock, it really isn't fair.
Knock, knock, I'm working all my charms.
Knock, knock, a zombie's in my arms.
All that sweet affection,
What is wrong?
Where's the loose connection?
How long, oh Lord, how long?
Bobby baby, Bobby bubi, Bobby,

You could drive a person buggy,
You could blow a person's cool.
Doo-doo doo-doo doo.
Like you make a person feel all huggy
While you make her feel a fool.
Doo-doo doo-doo doo.

When a person says that you've upset her,
That's when you're good.
You impersonate a person better
Than a zombie should.

I could understand a person
If he wasn't good in bed.
Doo-doo-doo-doo doo.
I could understand a person
If he actually was dead.
Doo-doo-doo-doo.

Exclusive you,
Elusive you,
Will any person ever get the juice of you?
You're crazy,

You're a lovely person,
You're a moving, deeply maladjusted,
Never to be trusted
Crazy person
Yourself.

(Spoken) Bobby is my hobby and I'm giving it up.

(They exit)

JENNY: I'm starving. I'll get us something to eat. Do one of you sons of bitches want to help? Then kiss my ass. *(She laughs)*

DAVID: Oh, boy.

JENNY: Did you light another one?

DAVID: Just a cigarette.

ROBERT: Shall I roll another one?

JENNY: Maybe one.

DAVID: No.

ROBERT: I can roll another one in a second.

DAVID: No.

ROBERT: No more?

DAVID: I don't think so.

(Pause)

JENNY: I don't think so either.

ROBERT: It'll just take a second to make another one.

(Pause)

DAVID: Listen, you two have one.

JENNY: I don't want one.

DAVID: Have one if you want one.

JENNY: But I don't.

(Pause)

I'll get some food. *(She embraces David)* Isn't he a marvelous man?

DAVID: I married a square. A confessed square.

(Jenny turns to exit, then turns back)

JENNY *(Seriously, to Robert)*: Bobby, we're just too old! We were all—trying to keep up with the kids tonight. Goodness, we've been there already. Who wants to go back? But anyway what do I know.

DAVID: Hey, screwball. I'm starving.

JENNY: I love you . . . so much.

DAVID: Food!

JENNY: And, Bobby. Put that stuff away. C'mon, put it in your pocket. Take it home. Come on.

(Robert does)

Thank you. I don't know. Maybe you're right. Who ever knows? *(She smiles and exits)*

ROBERT: What was all that?

DAVID: She doesn't go for it. I thought she wouldn't go for it.

ROBERT: She was stoned.

DAVID: Not really. She doesn't get things like that. I mean, she'll go along with it, but that's about it.

ROBERT: She didn't like it?

DAVID: I know her. She didn't.

(Pause)

ROBERT: You want me to get *you* some?

DAVID: She'd have a fit. I'm really surprised she did it tonight.

ROBERT: She loved it.

DAVID: For me. She loved it for me. She didn't really love it. I
    know her. She's what she said . . . square . . . dumb . . .

ROBERT: Like a fox.

*(Underscoring: "Bobby Baby" music. David pauses, then
looks at Robert. They stare at each other.)*

DAVID: I'll go see if I can give her a hand. What do you say?
    (He exits)

ROBERT: Wow. Oh, wow.

*(Robert starts to exit but is stopped by the couples who begin
to appear)*

JENNY:
    Bobby,

PETER:
    Bobby,

AMY:
    Bobby baby,

PAUL:
    Bobby bubi,

ALL BUT ROBERT:
    Robby,

SUSAN:
    Robert darling,

ALL BUT ROBERT:

>Bobby, we've been trying to reach you,

SARAH:

>Angel, I've got something to tell you . . .

AMY & PAUL:

>Bobby, it's important or I wouldn't call . . .

ALL BUT ROBERT:

>Whatcha doing Thursday?

JENNY & DAVID:

>Bobby, look I know how you hate it and all . . .

ALL BUT ROBERT:

>But this is something special.
>Bobby, come on over for dinner.
>There's someone we want you to meet.
>Bobby, come on over for dinner . . .

HUSBANDS:

>This girl from the office . . .

WIVES:

>My niece from Ohio . . .
>It'll just be the four of us . . .
>You'll looooooooooooooove her!

LARRY:

>Have I got a girl for you? Wait till you meet her!
>Have I got a girl for you, boy? Hoo, boy!
>Dumb—and with a weakness for Sazerac slings—
>You give her even the fruit and she swings.

The kind of girl you can't send through the mails—
Call me tomorrow, I want the details.

PETER:

Have I got a chick for you? Wait till you meet her!
Have I got a chick for you, boy? Hoo, boy!
Smart!—She's into all those exotic mystiques:
The Kama Sutra and Chinese techniques—
I hear she knows more than seventy-five . . .
Call me tomorrow if you're still alive.

HUSBANDS:

Have I got a girl for you? Wait till you meet her!
Have I got a girl for you, boy? Hoo, boy!
Boy, to be in your shoes what I wouldn't give.
I mean the freedom to go out and live . . .
And as for settling down and all that . . .
Marriage may be where it's been,
But it's not where it's at!

Whaddaya like, you like coming home to a kiss?
Somebody with a smile at the door?
Whaddaya like, you like indescribable bliss?
Then whaddaya wanna get married for?

Whaddaya like, you like an excursion to Rome,
Suddenly taking off to explore?
Whaddaya like, you like having meals cooked at home?
Then whaddaya wanna get married for?
Whaddaya wanna get married for?
Whaddaya wanna get married for?
Whaddaya wanna get married for?

(The husbands exit, leaving Robert alone onstage)

ROBERT:

> Someone is waiting,
> Cool as Sarah,
> Easy and loving as Susan—
> Jenny.
> Someone is waiting,
> Warm as Susan,
> Frantic and touching as Amy—
> Joanne.
>
> Would I know her even if I met her?
> Have I missed her? Did I let her go?
> A Susan sort of Sarah,
> A Jennyish Joanne,
> Wait for me, I'm ready now,
> I'll find you if I can!

(The women appear in dim light in various parts of the stage)

> Someone will hold me,
> Soft as Jenny,
> Skinny and blue-eyed as Amy—
> Susan.
> Someone will wake me,
> Sweet as Amy,
> Tender and foolish as Sarah,
> Joanne.
>
> Did I know her? Have I waited too long?
> Maybe so, but maybe so has she,
> My blue-eyed Sarah
> Warm Joanne
> Sweet Jenny
> Loving Susan

Crazy Amy,
Wait for me,
I'll hurry, wait for me.
Hurry.
Wait for me.
Hurry.
Wait.

Scene Five

Lights come up on Marta.

MARTA:

Another hundred people just got off of the train
    and came up through the ground
While another hundred people just got off of the bus
    and are looking around
At another hundred people who got off of the plane
    and are looking at us
Who got off of the train
And the plane and the bus
Maybe yesterday.

It's a city of strangers—
Some come to work, some to play—
A city of strangers—
Some come to stare, some to stay,
And everyday
The ones who stay

Can find each other in the crowded streets and the
    guarded parks,

> By the rusty fountains and the dusty trees with the
> battered barks,
> And they walk together past the postered walls with
> the crude remarks.
> And they meet at parties through the friends of
> friends
> Who they never know.
> Will you pick me up or do I meet you there or shall we
> let it go?
> Did you get my message, 'cause I looked in vain?
> Can we see each other Tuesday if it doesn't rain?
> Look, I'll call you in the morning or my service will
> explain . . .

And another hundred people just got off of the train.

*(April, in an airline stewardess' uniform, appears with
Robert. Marta observes the following scene)*

APRIL: I didn't come right to New York. I went to North-
western University for two years but it was a pitiful mis-
take. I was on probation the whole two years. I was getting ready to go back to Shaker Heights when I decided
where I really wanted to live more than any other place
was—Radio City. I thought it was a wonderful little city
near New York. So I came here. I'm very dumb.

ROBERT: You're not dumb, April.

APRIL: To me I am. Even the reason I stayed in New York was
because I just cannot get interested in myself—I'm so
boring.

ROBERT: I find you very interesting.

APRIL: Well, I'm just not. I used to think I was so odd. But my
roommate is the same way. He's also very dumb.

ROBERT: Oh, you never mentioned him. Is he—your lover?

APRIL: Oh, no. We just share this great big apartment on West End Avenue. We have our own rooms and everything. I'd show it to you but we've never had company. He's the sweetest thing actually. I think he likes the arrangement. I don't know though—we never discuss it. He was born in New York—so nothing really interests him. *(Pause)* I don't have anything more to say.

ROBERT: What would you do if either of you ever got married?

APRIL: Get a bigger place, I guess. *(She exits)*

MARTA:

> And they find each other in the crowded streets and the guarded parks,
> By the rusty fountains and the dusty trees with the battered barks,
> And they walk together past the postered walls with the crude remarks.
> And they meet at parties through the friends of friends Who they never know.
> Will you pick me up or do I meet you there or shall We let it go?
> Did you get my message, 'cause I looked in vain?
> Can we see each other Tuesday if it doesn't rain?
> Look, I'll call you in the morning or my service will explain . . .
> And another hundred people just got off of the train.

(Robert is now seen with Kathy)

ROBERT *(Putting her on)*: This is really exciting, Kathy. Fascinating.

KATHY: Robert, you are awful.

ROBERT: You come here a lot, huh? Terrific. And maybe next we can go watch a haircut.

KATHY: Oh, you cannot bear that with a big party going on I talked you into coming here with me.

ROBERT: What party are you—oh, *that* party. I'd completely forgotten about that party. But hey, maybe we can still make it.

KATHY: Robert, try to enjoy this. Imagine being in a tiny quiet pocket of a park right here in the middle of the busy, noisy East Fifties. A park that's simple and pretty, with that waterfall on the wall that always makes me ache to be back at the Cape.

ROBERT *(After a beat of looking at her)*: You are some piece of work, lady.

KATHY: What I am is like this park here. Out of place.

ROBERT: You are like this park. Very lovely. Very.

(As he leans in to kiss her she closes her eyes, but he only kisses her forehead in a brotherly way; she expected more)

KATHY: I used to dream I'd come to New York, have two terrific affairs and then get married. I always knew I was meant to be a wife.

ROBERT: Then how come *we* never got married? Why did you never ask me?

KATHY *(Turns. Right at him. Serious)*: You wanna marry me?

ROBERT: I did. I honestly did . . . in the beginning. But I . . . I don't know. I never thought that you would.

KATHY: Oh, I would. I've never understood why you never asked me.

ROBERT: So you wanted to marry me? And I wanted to marry you. Well then, how the hell did we ever end up such good friends?

KATHY: Robert, I never let you know what a good, good man I think you are and how much you've meant. Robert, I . . .

(She stops. Decides not to say it. Then:)

I brought you here because I wanted to tell you alone.
I'm moving back up to Cape Cod. I'm getting married.
ROBERT: Married?
KATHY: Some people still get married, you know.
ROBERT: Did you just suddenly fall in love?

(Pause. Then:)

KATHY: I'll be a good wife. I want real things now. A husband,
   a family. I don't want to keep running around this city
   like I'm having a life.
ROBERT: The problem is you want too little. That's the hardest
   thing in the world to get. *(Pause)* Thank you for your
   park.
KATHY: You're welcome. But, see, it and I, we just don't fit. I
   think there's a time to come to New York and a time to
   leave. Enjoy your party. *(And she is gone)*

MARTA:
>   Another hundred people just got off of the train
>   And came up through the ground
>   While another hundred people just got off of the bus
>   And are looking around
>   At another hundred people who got off of the plane
>   And are looking at us
>   Who got off of the train
>   And the plane and the bus
>   Maybe yesterday.
>
>   It's a city of strangers—
>   Some come to work, some to play.
>   A city of strangers—

Some come to stare, some to stay,
And everyday
Some go away . . .

Or they find each other in the crowded streets and the
   guarded parks,
By the rusty fountains and the dusty trees with the
   battered barks,
And they walk together past the postered walls with
   the crude remarks.
And they meet at parties through the friends of friends
Who they never know.
Will you pick me up or do I meet you there or shall
We let it go?
Did you get my message, 'cause I looked in vain?
Can we see each other Tuesday if it doesn't rain?
Look, I'll call you in the morning or my service will
   explain . . .

And another hundred people just got off of the train.

And another hundred people just got off of the train.
And another hundred people just got off of the train.
And another hundred people just got off of the train.
And another hundred people just got off of the train.

MARTA (*Sitting next to Robert*): You wanna know why I came
   to New York? I came because New York is the center of
   the world and that's where I want to be. You know what
   the pulse of this city is?
ROBERT: A busy signal.
MARTA: The pulse of this city, kiddo, is *me*. This city is for the
   me's of this world. People that want to be right in the
   heart of it. I am like the soul of New York.

ROBERT: How 'bout that.

MARTA: See, smart remarks do not a person make. How many Puerto Ricans you know?

ROBERT *(Thinking)*: Let's see . . . there's a guy at work . . . and uh . . .

MARTA *(Interrupting)*: How many blacks?

ROBERT: Well, see, frankly I only seem to meet people like myself.

MARTA: God, talk about pathetic. Jews, Hispanics, gays, Arabs, street people, all my closest, my best friends. Listen, I don't pass people on the street, I stop and I know them. In this city every son of a bitch I meet is my new best friend. Oh, I go uptown, like to the dentist or something, and I swear, suddenly I want to cry because I think, "Oh my God, I'm *uptown.*" And Fourteenth Street. Well, I don't know why anybody talks about anyplace *else,* because *that* is the center of the universe.

ROBERT: Fourteenth Street?

MARTA: That's humanity, Fourteenth Street. That's everything. And if you don't like it there they got every subway you can name to take ya where ya like it better.

ROBERT: Well, God bless Fourteenth Street.

MARTA: This city—I kiss the ground of it. Someday you know what I want to do? I want to get all dressed up in black—black dress, black shoes, hat, everything black, and go sit in some bar at the end of the counter, and drink and cry. That is my idea of honest-to-God sophistication. I mean, *that's* New York. *(Pause)* You always make me feel like I got the next line. What is it with you?

ROBERT: I just never met anybody like you.

MARTA: Me neither. You know what this city is? Where a person can feel it? It's in a person's ass. If you're really part of this city, relaxed, cool and in the whole flow of it, your ass is like this. *(She makes a large round circle with her fore-*

finger and thumb) If you're just living here, runnin' around uptight, not really part of this city, your ass is like this. *(She tightens the circle to nothing, making a fist)*

ROBERT: I . . . hesitate to ask.

(She holds up the "tight" sign high)

That's a fascinating theory, fascinating. And at this moment, extraordinarily accurate.

(Lights fade)

Scene Six

A woman (Susan or Jenny) in a white choir robe appears as lights come up on Amy's kitchen. The woman is accompanied by a choir of guests. Amy is shining a pair of men's black shoes.

WOMAN:

> Bless this day, pinnacle of life,
> Husband joined to wife.
> The heart leaps up to behold
> This golden day.

(Paul appears in dress shirt, shorts and socks)

PAUL: Amy, I can't find my shoes any—

> Today is for Amy.
> Amy, I give you the rest of my life,
> To cherish and to keep you,

To honor you forever.
Today is for Amy,
My happily soon-to-be wife.

(Spoken) Amy, we're really getting married!

(He exits; she shakes her head "yes" and it becomes "no")

AMY:

Pardon me, is everybody there?
Because if everybody's there
I want to thank you all for coming to the wedding.
I'd appreciate your going even more,
I mean, you must have lots of better things to do,
And not a word of it to Paul. Remember Paul?
You know, the man I'm gonna marry,
But I'm not because I wouldn't ruin
Anyone as wonderful as he is—

But I thank you all
For the gifts and the flowers.
Thank you all,
Now it's back to the showers.
Don't tell Paul,
But I'm not getting married today.

WOMAN:

Bless this day, tragedy of life,
Husband yolked to wife.
The heart sinks down and feels dead,
This dreadful day.

(Robert appears dressed as the Best Man)

ROBERT: Amy, Paul can't find his good cuff links.
AMY: On the dresser.

(Robert exits)

(Spoken) Right next to my suicide note.

Listen everybody,
Look, I don't know what you're waiting for.
A wedding, what's a wedding?
It's a prehistoric ritual
Where everybody promises fidelity forever,
Which is maybe the most horrifying word I've ever
     heard,
And which is followed by a honeymoon
Where suddenly he'll realize
He's saddled with a nut
And wanna kill me, which he should.

So listen,
Thanks a bunch,
But I'm not getting married.
Go have lunch,
'Cause I'm not getting married.
You've been grand,
But I'm not getting married.
Don't just stand
There, I'm not getting married.
And don't tell Paul,
But I'm not getting married today!

Go. Can't you go?
Why is nobody listening?
Goodbye! Go and cry

At another person's wake.
If you're quick, for a kick
You could pick up a christening,
But please, on my knees,
There's a human life at stake!

Listen, everybody, I'm afraid you didn't hear,
Or do you want to see a crazy lady
Fall apart in front of you?
It isn't only Paul who may be ruining his life, you
    know,
We'll both of us be losing our identities—
I telephoned my analyst about it
And he said to see him Monday,
But by Monday I'll be floating
In the Hudson with the other garbage.

I'm not well,
So I'm not getting married.
You've been swell,
But I'm not getting married.
Clear the hall,
'Cause I'm not getting married
Thank you all,
But I'm not getting married.
And don't tell Paul,
But I'm not getting married today.

WOMAN:

Bless this bride, totally insane,
Slipping down the drain,
And bless this day in our hearts—
As it starts to rain . . .

PAUL:	AMY:
Today is for Amy.	Go, can't you go?
Amy,	Look, you know
I give you	I adore you all,
The rest of my life,	But why watch me die
To cherish	Like Eliza on the ice?
And to keep	Look, perhaps
You,	I'll collapse
To honor you	In the apse
Forever.	Right before you all,
Today is for	So take back the cake,
Amy,	Burn the shoes and boil
	the rice!
My happily	
Soon-to-be	Look, I didn't want to
	have to tell you,
Wife,	But I may be coming down
	with hepatitis
	And I think I'm gonna faint,
	So if you wanna see me
	faint,
	I'll do it happily,
	But wouldn't it be funnier
	To go and watch a funeral?
	So thank you for the
	Twenty-seven dinner
	plates and
My	Thirty-seven butter
	knives and
Adorable	Forty-seven paper
	weights and
Wife.	Fifty-seven candle
	holders . . .

PAUL:

One more thing,

AMY:

I am not getting married!

WOMAN & GUESTS:
Amen.

PAUL:

Softly said:

AMY:

But I'm not getting married!

WOMAN & GUESTS:
Amen.

PAUL:

With this ring

AMY:

Still I'm not getting married!

WOMAN & GUESTS:
Amen.

PAUL:

I thee wed.

AMY:

See, I'm not getting married!

WOMAN & GUESTS:
Amen.

PAUL:	AMY:
Let us pray,	Let us pray
And we are	That I'm not
Getting married today.	Getting married today!

GROUP:
>Amen!

(Robert enters with the ring)

PAUL: Amy?

AMY: You're starting!

(Paul begins to speak)

Don't talk, please! Why don't the two of you sit down and talk to each other? I can't think with the two of you following me—everyplace I go—from the bedroom to the bathroom to the kitchen . . . I feel like I'm leading a parade. Paul, stop staring! I feel it—like bullets—right through my back. *(Without stopping)* No, Paul, please! I'm so crazy I left the refrigerator door open last night, so the orange juice is hot. Here, *(Offering him and Robert glasses of orange juice)* and if you say "thank you" I will go running right out of this apartment and move into the "hopeless cases" section at Bellevue where they'll understand me. Don't talk, please. *(Suddenly, she throws her arms around his neck and kisses him)* Oh, Paul. I apologize. Oh, Paul, you say whatever you wanna say. Whatever you like. Who am *I* telling *you* what to do? Oh, Paul.

(Pause)

PAUL: The orange juice is hot. But thanks.

AMY: Paul, see! You don't thank a person for hot orange juice! You slug 'em.

(Smoke rises from the toaster)

The toast! *(She takes two charred pieces of toast out of the toaster and throws them onto breakfast plates)* Now, I blew the toast.

PAUL: That's okay.

AMY: I can't stand it! IT'S NOT OKAY, PAUL. NOTHING ABOUT IT EVEN REMOTELY RESEMBLES OKAY. IT IS THE OPPOSITE OF OKAY. Oh, Robert, this is the real me. Crazed!

ROBERT: I was just thinking that this is probably a much more interesting wedding breakfast than most. And, uh, that the bride is in a high-energy mode. The groom is abnormally quiet. But yet a festive atmosphere pervades the room—I guess it's the Best Man, smiling, even as he dies from drinking boiled orange juice.

AMY: I would laugh, Robert, if it weren't all so tragic. How do I look? Funny?

PAUL: Yeah, that's a funny dress.

AMY: That dumb hairdresser curled my hair like he was on withdrawal. Paul, what are you so happy about all the time?

PAUL: You.

AMY: This is the most neurotic . . . insane . . . it is . . . so *crazy* having this enormous wedding and everything after we've been living together all these years! It's embarrassing, Paul. People will think I'm pregnant.

PAUL: That's next year. Listen, if we hurry, we're late.

AMY: What am I doing? I'm thirty-one.

PAUL: And perfect.

AMY: Oh. An oldie but a goodie, huh? It's just incredible. Two years with a psychiatrist . . . and look where it leads. I am just so glad we're not having a Catholic wedding because next year when I get the divorce I won't be a sinner. Whoever would have thought I'd *marry* someone Jewish? Jewish! I mean I didn't even *know* anybody who was Jewish. See, Robert. That was probably my main attraction. Look what a little Catholic rebellion will lead to! The very first moment I met Paul, I said to myself, "That's what I really like . . . that Jew!" Oh, he was so beautiful . . . inside and out beautiful. Paul would kiss me and I would think, "Oh, I got my very own Jew!"

PAUL: What is all this about me being Jewish today? About three-quarters of your friends are Jewish. Hurry.

AMY: Did I ever say I like my friends. I do not. I much prefer my Gentile enemies, at least they leave you alone. And I need to be left alone. I'm just like Robert.

ROBERT: I'm not like *that!* What the hell are you talking about? But don't answer, because we don't have time.

PAUL: Amy. After all these years, don't you know we fit.

AMY: The higher you go, the harder you hurt when you fall.

PAUL: I never dropped you yet.

(She goes to take a sip of coffee, sees a note in the saucer, then shows the saucer to Robert. Robert opens the note)

ROBERT: "Whoever reads this . . . I love you." Well, thank you, I love *you.*

AMY: Thank him. The phantom. He leaves notes like that all over the place. A person can't stand all that sweetness, Paul. Nobody human can stand all that everlasting affection.

PAUL: Amy, don't you think we should go?

AMY: I can't.

PAUL: Amy, if anybody should be married, it's you. Tell her, Robert.

AMY: Robert tell me? Who's going to tell Robert?

(Pause)

ROBERT: Paul, I can't tell anybody anything like that. I guess whatever is right will happen.

(Pause)

PAUL: I see.

ROBERT: Listen, I'm going to call and say that, ah . . . that . . . that we'll be late. That we'll be a little late. The people will be getting there, don't you think? *(He exits)*

PAUL: Amy, do you see what you're doing to yourself? Do you know if other people did to you what you do to yourself, they could be put in jail? C'mon.

(Sounds of thunder)

AMY: Oh, Paul, look . . . oh, look . . . it's starting to rain.

(Robert enters)

ROBERT: It's starting to rain. The line's busy . . . Oh, guess who I ran into coming over here today. Helen Kincaid? Remember Helen Kincaid? I brought her around a few times. Well, she's married now. I almost didn't recognize her, all fat and blowsy and . . . *(Realizing their dismayed reaction, stops)*

PAUL: Amy. C'mon. We're late.

AMY: I can't do it, Paul. I don't understand how I ever let it get this far.

(Sounds of thunder again)

Oh look, will you look at that, now it's really starting to rain . . . look at it . . . it's a flood, it's a sign; thank you God, now explain it to him!

PAUL: Amy, let's go. All our friends are waiting.

AMY: That's no reason, Paul. I just can't. I'm so afraid.

PAUL: Of what?

AMY: I don't know. I don't know. I just think you're really not for me, Paul. I just think maybe nobody's for me. I never saw one good marriage. Never. Not in my entire life.

PAUL: You just see what you look for, you know. I've seen a lot. Listen, Amy . . . married people are no more *marriage* than . . . oh . . . musicians are music. Just because some of the people might be wrong—doesn't matter . . . *it* is still *right*.

AMY: Yes, well, I'll put that on a sampler, Paul. *(She looks up; right to Paul)* Please. I'm not being emotional. I'm as sane as can be. Paul? I'm sorry. I don't love you *enough*.

(There is a very long pause)

PAUL: Robert . . . would you . . . call and ah . . . explain and . . . I'm . . . I ah, I . . . *(He exits)*

AMY: What did I just do?

ROBERT: You did . . . what you had to do . . . I guess . . . if it was right, you would have gone through with it. That's what I think, anyway. Amy, marry me.

AMY: What?

ROBERT: Marry me.

(Underscoring: "Bobby Baby" music)

AMY: Huh?

ROBERT: You said it before—we're just alike. Why don't we, Amy?

AMY: Why don't we, Robert?

COMPANY *(Voice-over)*:
> Bobby, Bobby,
> Bobby, baby, Bobby bubi,
> Bobby . . .

ROBERT: Marry me! And everybody'll leave us alone!

COMPANY *(Voice-over)*:
> Bobby . . . Bobby . . . how have you been?
> Stop by on your way home . . .
> Bobby, we've been thinking of you . . .

AMY: Isn't this some world? I'm afraid to get married and you're afraid not to. Thank you, Robert. I'm really . . . it's just that you have to want to marry *some*body, not just some*body*.

(Sounds of thunder again. Amy notices Paul's rain clothes)

Oh! Would you look at that! He went out without an umbrella or anything. *(She puts on a raincoat and grabs another coat and umbrella for Paul)*

He'll get pneumonia. I've got to catch him. I'm getting married. Oh, and he's so good, isn't he? So good. *(She starts to exit)*

ROBERT: Amy!

(He throws her the bouquet; Amy catches it and holds it in front of her)

AMY: I'm the next bride. *(She exits)*

COMPANY *(Voice-over)*:
>Bobby, come on over for dinner!
>Just be the three of us,
>Only the three of us,
>We looooooooooooove . . .

ROBERT:
>Marry me a little,
>Love me just enough.
>Cry, but not too often,
>Play, but not too rough.
>
>Keep a tender distance,
>So we'll both be free.
>That's the way it ought to be.
>I'm ready!
>
>Marry me a little,
>Do it with a will.
>Make a few demands
>I'm able to fulfill.
>
>Want me more than others,
>Not exclusively.
>That's the way it ought to be.
>I'm ready!
>I'm ready now!
>
>You can be my best friend.
>I can be your right arm.
>We'll go through a fight or two.
>No harm, no harm.

We'll look not too deep,
We'll go not too far.
We won't have to give up a thing,
We'll stay who we are.
Right?

Okay, then, I'm ready!
I'm ready now!

Someone, marry me a little,
Love me just enough.
Warm and sweet and easy,
Just the simple stuff.

Keep a tender distance
So we'll both be free.
That's the way it ought to be.
I'm ready!

Marry me a little,
Body, heart and soul.
Passionate as hell,
But always in control.

Want me first and foremost,
Keep me company.
That's the way it ought to be.
I'm ready!
I'm ready now!

Oh, how gently we'll talk,
Oh, how softly we'll tread.
All the stings, the ugly things
We'll keep unsaid.

We'll build a cocoon of love and respect.
You promise whatever you like,
I'll never collect.
Right?

Okay, then, I'm ready!
I'm ready now!—Someone . . .
I'm ready! I'm ready! I'm ready!

COUPLES *(Voice-over)*:
Bobby, Bobby,
Bobby baby, Bobby bubi,
Bobby . . .

Bobby, Bobby,
Bobby baby, Bobby bubi,
Bobby . . .

(Lights come up on all the birthday guests looking at Robert as in Act One, Scene One. Robert stares at Amy as she enters with the cake and the music builds. They blow out the candles.)

CURTAIN

ACT TWO

Scene One

Robert's apartment.

COUPLES:

> Bobby, Bobby,
> Ba ba ba ba ba ba ba ba.
> Bobby, Bobby,
> Ba ba ba ba ba ba ba ba
> Bobby . . .

(Lights come up on the birthday party with Robert about to blow out the candles and all five couples standing around him. As the scene progresses, the pace accelerates)

AMY: Well, our blessings, Robert.

JENNY: Don't tell your wish, Bobby, or it won't come true.

(Robert blows out most of the candles. The others blow out the rest hurriedly. All ad lib "Awww," etc.)

JOANNE: You just blew it.

AMY: It probably was a wish you wouldn't have got anyway, Robert.

DAVID: You wish for a wife, Robert?

PETER: Don't. You're a lucky son of a gun now. Hang in there.

SARAH: Stay exactly the same. You may be the one constant in this world of variables.

HARRY: I don't know, Sarah, you can't stay in your thirties forever.

JENNY: You'll still get your wish, Bobby.

JOANNE: Won't.

SUSAN: I think he still gets his wish.

JOANNE: I say he won't.

LARRY: Joanne, come on. See, when she and Robert get together . . .

JOANNE: Larry, I'm telling you, if you do not blow out all the candles on the cake, you do not get your wish. I know all the rules for birthday candle blowing out, I've had enough for a wax museum.

ROBERT: All right, all right! Actually, I didn't wish for anything.

DAVID: What do you mean you didn't wish for . . .

SUSAN *(Interrupting)*: Oh, tell, everybody's so curious.

PETER: Tell, but lie.

ROBERT: Thank you for including me in your thoughts, your lives.

(All other characters exit on their following lines, leaving Robert alone)

PAUL: Stay exactly as you are, Robert.

SARAH: That's right, you sweet thing, you stay exactly as you are.

(Underscoring: "Bobby Baby" music)

JOANNE: Everyone adores you. What an awful thing. I'd kiss you goodnight, Robby, but Larry gets jealous.

AMY: Things always happen for the best. I don't even believe that myself.

ROBERT *(Shouting after them)*: I mean, when you've got friends like mine . . .

("Side by Side by Side" introduction starts softly)

(Spoken) I mean, when you've got friends like mine . . .

> Isn't it warm,
> Isn't it rosy,
> Side by side . . .

SARAH *(Entering)*: He's such a cutie.

ROBERT:
> . . . by side?

SARAH: Isn't he a cutie?

ROBERT:
> Ports in a storm,
> Comfy and cozy,
> Side by side . . .

PETER *(Entering)*: He never loses his cool.

ROBERT:
> . . . by side?

HARRY *(Entering)*: I envy that.

ROBERT:
> Everything shines.
> How sweet . . .

(Jenny and David enter)

ROBERT, JENNY & DAVID:
    Side by side . . .

SUSAN *(Entering)*: We're just so fond of him.

ROBERT:
    . . . by side.
    Parallel lines
    Who meet . . .

(Amy, Paul and Susan enter)

AMY, PAUL, PETER, SUSAN, SARAH, HARRY, DAVID & JENNY:
    Love him—
    Can't get enough of him.

ROBERT:
    Everyone winks,
    Nobody's nosy,
    Side by side . . .

JOANNE *(Entering)*: He's just crazy about me.

ROBERT:
    . . . by side.

PAUL: He's a very tender guy.

ROBERT:
    You bring the drinks and
    I'll bring the posy . . .

(Larry enters)

ROBERT, LARRY & JOANNE:
    Side by side . . .

LARRY: He's always there when you need him.

ROBERT:
    . . . by side.
    One is lonely and two is boring,
    Think what you can keep ignoring.
    Side . . .

AMY: He's my best friend.

ROBERT:
    . . . by side . . .

(Paul and others look at Amy)

AMY *(Touching Paul)*: Second-best.

ROBERT:
    . . . by side.

COUPLES:
    Never a bother,
    Seven times a godfather.

ROBERT, AMY & PAUL:
    Year after year,
    Older and
    Older . . .

LARRY: It's amazing. We've gotten older every year and he seems to stay exactly the same.

ALL:

> Sharing a tear,
> Lending a shoulder.

DAVID: You know what comes to my mind when I see him? The Seagram's Building. Isn't that funny?

ROBERT, PETER, SUSAN, SARAH & HARRY:

> Ain't we got fun?
> No strain . . .

JOANNE: Sometimes I catch him looking and looking. And I just look right back.

COUPLES:

> Permanent sun, no rain . . .
> We're so crazy, he's so sane.
> Friendship forbids
> Anything bitter . . .

PAUL: A person like Bob doesn't have the good things and he doesn't have the bad things. But he doesn't have the good things.

COUPLES:

> Being the kids
> As well as the sitter . . .

HARRY: Let me make him a drink. He's the only guy I know, I feel should drink more.

ROBERT:

>One's impossible, two is dreary,
>Three is company, safe and cheery,

ROBERT & SARAH:

>Side . . .

SARAH:

>He always looks like he's keeping score.

ROBERT:

>. . . by side . . .

SARAH: Who's winning, Robert?

ROBERT:

>. . . by side.

ROBERT:

>Here is the church,
>Here is the steeple
>Open the doors and
>See all the crazy, married people!

COUPLES:

>What would we do without you?
>How would we ever get through?
>Who would I complain to for hours?
>Who'd bring me the flowers
>When I have the flu?
>Who'd finish yesterday's stew?
>Who'd take the kids to the zoo?

Who is so dear?
And who is so deep?
And who would keep her/him occupied
When I want to sleep?
How would we ever get through?
What would we do without you?

(Dance break)

(Out of breath) Huff. Huff. Huff. Huff.

What would we do without you?
How would we ever get through?
Should there be a marital squabble,
Available Bob'll
Be there with the glue.
Who could we open up to,
Secrets we keep from guess-who?

Who is so safe and who is so sound?
You never need an analyst with Bobby around.
How could we ever get through?
What would we do without you?

(Parade dance break. Top hat section)

What would we do without you?
How would we ever get through?
Who sends anniversary wishes?
Who helps with the dishes
And never says boo?
Who changes subjects on cue?
Who cheers us up when we're blue?

Who is a flirt but never a threat,
Reminds us of our birthdays which we always forget?
How would we ever get through?
What would we do without you?

(Robert hides as couples look for him. He is found and dragged back into the number)

ROBERT: Huff. Huff. Huff. Huff.

COUPLES:

What would we do without you?
How would we ever get . . .
How would we ever get . . .
How would we ever get . . .
How would we ever get . . . through?
What would we do without you?

ROBERT:

Just what you usually do!

COUPLES:

Right!
You who sit with us . . .
You who share with us . . .
You who fit with us . . .
You who bear with us . . .
You-who, you-hoo, you-hoo,
You-hoo, you-hoo . . .

ROBERT: Okay, now everybody—!

ALL:

Isn't it warm, isn't it rosy,
Side by side?

(Harry does a brief dance break, answered by Sarah)

Ports in a storm, comfy and cozy,
Side by side?

(Paul does a brief dance break, answered by Amy)

Everything shines, how sweet,
Side by side?

(Larry does a brief dance break, answered by Joanne)

Parallel lines who meet,
Side by side.

(Robert does a brief dance break, answered by total silence. He stands stunned as the others look at him; after a brief pause, they continue singing vigorously)

Year after year, older and older,
Side by side.
Sharing a tear and lending a shoulder,
Side by side.
Two's impossible, two is gloomy,
Give another number to me.
Side by side,
By side,

By side, by side, by side, by side, by side,
By side, by side, by side, by side, by side,

By side!

(All couples exit leaving Robert alone onstage. April enters)

Scene Two

Robert's apartment. April enters wearing her stewardess' uniform; she appears self-conscious, as this is her first visit.

APRIL: Oh! It's a darling apartment.

ROBERT: Thank you.

APRIL: Just darling. Did you do it yourself?

ROBERT: Me? Yes, I did, yes.

APRIL: Yourself?

ROBERT: Yes.

APRIL: Really?

ROBERT: Yes.

APRIL: Well, it's darling. Did you really do it all yourself?

ROBERT: Yes! Why? Did you hear I didn't?

APRIL: No, but look. This! This is just precious.

ROBERT: It is, isn't it? I never really look at it. I just—live here.

APRIL: Oh, it's terribly clever. *(Doing the stewardess' two-finger wave forward and back as she demonstrates)* See how nicely all the furniture is placed in areas to make it so warm and sweet and tucked in.

ROBERT: How about that?

APRIL: And the choice of colors is so relaxing and simple and masculine.

ROBERT: See that!

APRIL: Isn't that tasteful and interesting?

ROBERT: Yes. I'll take it. I mean I've always liked my apartment but I'm never really in it. I just seem to pass through the living room on my way to the bedroom to go to the bathroom to get ready to go out again.

APRIL: You never really spend any time in here? And it's so dear. But maybe that's why you like it so much. If you don't spend much time in it, it keeps it special and important.

ROBERT *(Amazed)*: Yes. *(Slowly)* And this is the bedroom over here.

(She crosses to it)

You love it, I can tell. Well, I can always look for another place.

(April looks up at the ceiling, where she sees a mirror. Embarrassed, she looks away, adjusting her hair. Robert shrugs. Then, he begins making love to her.
The lights come up on Sarah and Harry)

SARAH:

Darling—

HARRY:

Yes?

SARAH:

Robert—

HARRY:

What?

SARAH:

I worry—

HARRY:

Why?

SARAH:

He's all alone.

(Harry grunts)

There's no one—

HARRY:

Where?

SARAH:

In his life.

HARRY:

Oh.

SARAH:

Robert ought to have a woman.

Poor baby, all alone,
Evening after evening by the telephone—
We're the only tenderness he's ever known.
Poor baby . . .

(Lights come up on Jenny and David)

JENNY:

David—

DAVID:

Yes?

JENNY:

Bobby—

DAVID:

What?

JENNY:

    I worry.

DAVID:

    Why?

JENNY:

    It's such a waste.

(David grunts)

    There's no one.

DAVID:

    Where?

JENNY:

    In his life.

DAVID:

    Oh.

JENNY:

    Bobby ought to have a woman.
    Poor baby, sitting there,
    Staring at the walls and playing solitaire,
    Making conversation with the empty air—
    Poor baby.

APRIL: Right after I became an airline stewardess, a friend of mine who had a garden apartment gave me a cocoon for my bedroom. He collects things like that, insects and caterpillars and all that . . . It was attached to a twig and he said one morning I'd wake up to a beautiful butterfly in my bedroom—when it hatched. He told me that when they come out they're soaking wet and there is a drop of blood there, too—isn't that fascinating—but within an hour they dry off and then they begin to fly. Well, I told him I had a cat. I had a cat then, but he said just put the cocoon somewhere where the cat couldn't get at it . . . which is impossible, but what can you do? So I put it up high on a ledge where the cat never went, and the next morning it was still there, at least so it seemed safe to leave it. Well, anyway, almost a week later very, very early this one morning the guy calls me, and he said, "April, do you have a butterfly this morning?" I told him to hold on and managed to get up and look and there on that ledge I saw this wet spot and a little speck of blood but no butterfly, and I thought "Oh dear God in heaven, the cat got it." I picked up the phone to tell this guy and just then suddenly I spotted it under the dressing table, it was moving one wing. The cat had got at it, but it was still alive. So I told the guy and he got so upset and he said "Oh no—oh, God, no—don't you see that's a life—a living thing?" Well, I got dressed and took it to the park and put it on a rose, it was summer then, and it looked like it was going to be all right—I think, anyway. But that man—I really felt damaged by him—awful— that was just cruel. I got home and I called him back and said, "Listen, I'm a living thing too, you shithead!" *(Pause)* I never saw him again.

(Robert stands staring, pause)

ROBERT: That reminds me of something I did to someone once . . . in Miami . . . I mean it's not really the same but in a way. Well, you'll see. I met a girl, a lovely girl, at a party one night and, well, it was like you and me, April.

We just—connected. You don't mind my telling this, do you?

APRIL: No.

ROBERT: It just . . . came to my mind. Anyway, we just connected, in such a beautiful way . . . exactly like tonight. Except we couldn't even contain ourselves. It was incredible. We were talking and suddenly we realized we just couldn't talk anymore. No sounds came. We stood looking at each other and we were both bathed in perspiration. Our breathing was so short and our legs were trembling and we just left. We drove to one of those strips there where they have all those motels, and we didn't even say anything. She just sat so close to me. So close. We got inside that room and we started touching and kissing and laughing and holding and suddenly she said I should go get lots of Champagne and some baby oil and we should get beautifully high and then rub . . . well, you know. She said she'd be in bed waiting for me.

(April is visibly being turned on by this story)

I rushed out of there and I drove around until I could find a liquor store and a drugstore open and I got all this Champagne and the oil and finally I started back to the motel and—I—could not—find—it.

(April reacts)

I looked for over three hours. I never found it. And I never saw her again either.

APRIL *(Her breathing heavy)*: Oh. That is the most extraordinary story I have ever heard.

(Robert helps her out of her jacket)

That poor, poor girl. And you drove around for three hours?

(Robert unzips April's blouse and almost absentmindedly she takes off her skirt. He begins undressing her rapidly, then drops his own clothes and tosses them next to the bed. He pulls back the bedspread on both sides. April sits on the bed and unrolls her stockings)

ROBERT: More! All night I tried to find that motel. I mean all night. With the oil and all that Champagne and my hands trembling and sweat running down my face.

(April, close to tears, is under the covers now; Robert joins her under the covers, completing his undressing on the other side of the bed)

APRIL: Oh, that girl. She never knew. Oh. Well, I just don't know what to say or do. That is so sad!
ROBERT: I know. It is. Very.

(On the bed, they begin to make love; suddenly April stops and sits up)

APRIL: But Robert. Those stories don't really follow. I don't see the connection. Unless . . . oh . . . you must have thought of that poor girl as the wounded butterfly . . .

(Robert looks up to the sky with a "thank you" expression)

ROBERT: Yes! That's it!

(In a split second they're both under the covers again as lights go down on the bedroom and come up on Sarah and Jenny)

SARAH:

> Robert . . .

JENNY:

> Bobby . . .

SARAH:

> Robert, angel . . .

JENNY:

> Bobby, honey . . .

SARAH:

> You know, no one
> Wants you to be happy
> More than I do,
> No one, but
> Isn't she a little bit, well,
> You know . . ?
> Face it. Why her?
> Better, no one . . .

JENNY:

> You know . . .
> No one . . .

JENNY:

> Wants you to be happy
> More than I do.
> No one, but . . .

SARAH & JENNY:

> Isn't she a little bit, well
> You know,
> Face it.

SUSAN *(Entering)*:

> You know, no one

Wants you to be happy
More then I do.

AMY & JOANNE *(Entering)*:
You know, no one
Wants you to be happy
More than I do. No one, but . . .

ALL WOMEN:
Isn't she a little bit, well . . .

SARAH:
Dumb? Where is she from?

AMY:
Tacky? Neurotic? She seems so dead.

(Simultaneous)

SUSAN:
Vulgar? Aggressive? Peculiar?

JENNY:
Old? And cheap and . . .

JOANNE:
Tall? She's tall enough to be your mother

SARAH:
She's very weird . . .

JENNY:
Gross and . . .

(Simultaneous)

SUSAN:
Depressing, and . . .

AMY:
>
> And immature . . .

JOANNE:
>
> Goliath . . .

ALL WOMEN:
>
> Poor baby,
> All alone
> Throw a lonely dog a bone,
> It's still a bone.
> We're the only tenderness
> He's ever known.
> Poor baby.

(The five husbands enter from various parts of the stage near and around the darkened bed)

FIVE HUSBANDS:
>
> Have I got a girl for you? Wait till you meet her!
> Have I got a girl for you, boy? Hoo, boy . . .

(The men, holding the last note, exit, as lights come up on the bedroom as before. Music starts as April gets up and begins dressing. Robert, just waking up, sees this and sleepily sings:)

ROBERT:
>
> Where you going?

APRIL:
>
> Barcelona.

ROBERT:
>
> . . . oh . . .

APRIL:

Don't get up.

ROBERT:

Do you have to?

APRIL:

Yes, I have to.

ROBERT:

... oh ...

APRIL:

Don't get up.

(Pause)

Now you're angry.

ROBERT:

No, I'm not.

APRIL:

Yes, you are.

ROBERT:

No, I'm not.
Put your things down.

APRIL:

See, you're angry.

ROBERT:

No, I'm not.

APRIL:

    Yes, you are.

ROBERT:

    No, I'm not.
    Put your wings down
    And stay.

APRIL:

    I'm leaving.

ROBERT:

    Why?

APRIL:

    To go to—

ROBERT:

    Stay.

APRIL:

    I have to—

BOTH:

    Fly—

ROBERT:

    I know,

BOTH:

    To Barcelona.

ROBERT:

    Look,
    You're a very special girl,

Not just overnight.
No, you're a very special girl,

(Yawning)

And not because you're bright—
Not *just* because you're bright.
You're just a very special girl,
June!

APRIL:

April . . .

ROBERT:

April . . .

(Pause)

APRIL:

Thank you.

ROBERT:

Whatcha thinking?

APRIL:

Barcelona.

ROBERT:

. . . oh . . .

APRIL:

Flight 18.

ROBERT:

Stay a minute.

APRIL:

> I would like to.

ROBERT:

> . . . so? . . .

APRIL:

> Don't be mean.

ROBERT:

> Stay a minute.

APRIL:

> No, I can't.

ROBERT:

> Yes, you can.

APRIL:

> No, I can't.

ROBERT:

> Where you going?

APRIL:

> Barcelona.

ROBERT:

> So you said.

APRIL:

> And Madrid.

ROBERT:

> Bon voyage.

APRIL:

> On a Boeing.

ROBERT:

> Good night.

APRIL:

> You're angry.

ROBERT:

> No.

APRIL:

> I've got to—

ROBERT:

> Right.

APRIL:

> Report to—

ROBERT:

> Go.

APRIL:

> That's not to
> Say
> That if I had my way . . .
> Oh well, I guess okay.

ROBERT:

> What?

APRIL:

> I'll stay.

ROBERT:

But . . .

(As she snuggles down)

Oh, God.

(Blackout)

Scene Three

Peter and Susan are cleaning and fixing up the terrace as Robert and Marta enter.

SUSAN: Bobby, what a nice surprise. Peter, look who dropped in. Oh, I know, you must be Kathy.

MARTA: Wrong.

PETER: April? Shelly?

SUSAN *(As Marta continues to shake her head "no")*: KiKi? Nancy?

ROBERT: Whoa. See, they're great kidders. This is Marta.

SUSAN: Oh, Marta, of course, and you're just what Robert said. So pretty and so—original.

MARTA *(Leaning over the railing)*: Oh, cool, look. You can see the East River.

ROBERT *(Pulling her back after Susan reacts badly)*: Well, I'm real surprised to find you two guys out on your terrace.

PETER: Oh, I decided to fix it all up.

SUSAN *(To Marta)*: Is our Robert not a thing of beauty and a boy forever?

PETER: So, how you been, Bob?

ROBERT: Oh, you know me, always happy.

(The other three have been looking away; now they drop their smiles and turn to Robert)

PETER *(Covering the awkward moment)*: Yo, Bob, did Susan ever show the terrific pictures from Mexico when I went down to get the divorce?

ROBERT: Divorce? You mean you two are not married now?

SUSAN: Well, not since the divorce.

PETER: It was so absolutely sensational I phoned Susan to come down and join me.

SUSAN: We both put on five pounds.

ROBERT: Then where are you living now, Peter?

PETER: Why, here at home. I mean, I've got responsibilities. I've got Susan and the kids to take care of. I certainly would never leave them.

ROBERT: So, are you two considering getting married again?

SUSAN: Married? Oh, no, we tried that, thank you very much.

PETER: We're so much more married now than when we were married.

ROBERT: Well, I guess it takes two to make a happy divorce.

SUSAN: Whenever Robert's over I get this feeling we're auditioning for him.

ROBERT: Well, you know my favorite quote . . . "The unexamined life is not worth living."

PETER: And I think mine is . . . *(Pointing at Robert)* "The unlived life is not worth examining."

SUSAN *(Turning to exit)*: Why don't I skedaddle inside and I'll fix us a quick lunch. *(Turns back)* Look, we're all four single. It's nicer, I think. *(Taking Peter's arm)* Especially if you have someone.

ROBERT *(Aside, to Marta)*: I know. This is why you love New York.

MARTA *(Shooting a fist)*: Yes!!

SUSAN: Oh, Marta, come, so we can talk about you-know-who. *(She takes Marta's hand and leads her off)*

PETER: She's terrific, Robert. *(Pause)* Are you excited about the younger generation?

ROBERT: At moments.

PETER: Jesus, Robert, this is when *I* should be being born. This is *my* age. Wild-ass kids with probing minds rebelling against all the crap. I identify with those kids.

ROBERT: Shouldn't. You're the enemy the same as their parents.

PETER: No, sir, not I.

ROBERT: Peter, we're square to those kids.

PETER: Robert, did you ever have a homosexual experience?

ROBERT: I beg your pardon?

PETER: Oh, I don't mean as a kid. I mean, since you've been adult. Have you ever?

ROBERT: Well, yes, actually, yes, I have.

PETER: You're not gay, are you?

ROBERT: No, no. Are you?

PETER: No, no, for crissake. But I've done it more than once though.

ROBERT: Is that a fact?

PETER: Oh, I think sometimes you meet somebody and you just love the crap out of them. Y'know?

ROBERT: Oh, absolutely, I'm sure that's true.

PETER: And sometimes you just want to manifest that love, that's all.

ROBERT: Yes, I understand. Absolutely.

PETER: I think that sometimes you can even know someone for, oh, a long, long time and then suddenly, out of nowhere, you just want to have them—I mean, even an old friend. You just, all of a sudden, desire that intimacy. That closeness.

ROBERT: Probably.

PETER: Oh, I'm convinced that two men really would, if it wasn't for society and all the conventions and all that crap, just go off and ball and be better off for it, closer, deeper, don't you think?

ROBERT: Well, I—I don't know.

PETER: I mean like us, for example. Do you think that you and I could ever have anything like that?

ROBERT *(Looks at him for a long and uncomfortable moment. Then a big smile)*: Oh, I get it. You're putting me on. Man, you really had me going there, you son of a gun.

(Laughing, Robert points at Peter and exits. Peter, alone, opens his mouth to call after him but doesn't. Peter exits. Blackout)

Scene Four

The stage is alive with the activity of a private club.

Joanne and Robert are watching Joanne's husband Larry dance with one of the patrons. After Joanne and Robert watch them dance awhile, drinks arrive at Joanne's table, and she turns to Robert. Dance music softens.

Joanne and Robert grow increasingly drunk as the scene progresses. Larry is quite sober.

ROBERT: I think they're going to hurt themselves.

JOANNE: What if their mothers came in and saw them up there doing that. Think of their poor mothers. He's embarrassing.

ROBERT: Anyway, those people that laugh and carry on and dance like that—they're not happy.

JOANNE *(Yelling in Larry's direction)*: Think of your poor mother!

ROBERT: He's not what you'd call self-conscious.

JOANNE: He's not what you'd call! Big show-off. It really shocks me to see a grown man dance like that! I am shocked, you hear, shocked! Where was I? Oh—my first husband. He is so difficult to remember. Even when you're with him. We got married here in New York. I was just out of college. See. He was here on some business deal, but he owned a big meat-packing company in Chicago. Attractive? Well, we lived in New York for almost a year and then one day he had to go back to Chicago. And you know, he was actually surprised when I told him I would just wait here for him. I mean, I still really don't know quite where Chicago is. It's over there somewhere. *(She points front)* He said he didn't really plan to come back . . . so I knew we were in a tiny dilemma—or at least he was. I was still too young. But I was old enough to know where I was living, and I had no intention of leaving New York. I have never left New York. Never have, never will. And least of all would I ever want to go to a place where they actually feel honored being called "hog butchers to the world." They're proud of that! I said, "Kiss off, Rodney," but I said it nicer. Well, we got a divorce. A divorce. Huh—! One word means all of that. *(Calling to a passing waiter)* Another drink, guy . . . sir. OH, SIR!

(The waiter ignores her. The dance ends; Larry and the patron say goodbye and he crosses to Joanne)

LARRY: Whew!

JOANNE *(Looking up at him and away)*: We already gave.

LARRY: You all had a few while I was dancing, huh?

JOANNE: Larry, what the hell was all that carrying on? What was that? Shocking.

LARRY: I asked you to dance.

JOANNE: I only dance when you can touch. I don't think standing bumping around and making an ass out of oneself is a dance. I find it unbelievably humiliating watching my own husband flouncing around the dance floor, jerking and sashaying all over the place like Ann Miller. Take off the red shoes, Larry. Off.

LARRY *(To Robert)*: Was I that good?

ROBERT: Very. Excellent. Amazingly good.

LARRY: Joanne, I love it when you're jealous. Kiss me.

JOANNE: I hated dinner. I hated the opera, and I hate it here. What I need is more to drink—and look at Bobby, how desperately he needs another drink.

(The waiter enters again)

SIR. TWO MORE BOURBONS AND A VODKA STINGER! SIR! *(To Larry and Robert)* Do you know that we are suddenly at an age where we find ourselves too young for the old people and too old for the young ones. We're nowhere. I think we better drink to us. To us—the generation gap. *(She yells at the other women sitting in the club)* WE ARE THE GENERATION GAP! *(To Larry and Robert)* Are they staring at me? Let 'em stare—let 'em, those broads. What else have they got to do—all dressed up with no place to go.

LARRY: What time is it?

JOANNE: In real life? Will somebody get us another drink!

(Just then, the waiter delivers them)

Oh, you did. So aggressive. *(To the other women)* STOP
STARING!

*(She picks up her drink, puts it to her lips, doesn't drink, puts
it down, as lights fade on the nightclub)*

I'd like to propose a toast. *(Raises the glass again and
sings to the audience:)*

> Here's to the ladies who lunch . . .
> Everybody laugh.
> Lounging in their caftans and planning a brunch
> On their own behalf.
> Off to the gym,
> Then to a fitting,
> Claiming they're fat.
> And looking grim
> 'Cause they've been sitting
> Choosing a hat—
> Does anyone still wear a hat?
> I'll drink to that.

(Drinks)

> Here's to the girls who stay smart—
> Aren't they a gas?
> Rushing to their classes in optical art,
> Wishing it would pass.
> Another long exhausting day,
> Another thousand dollars,
> A matinee, a Pinter play,
> Perhaps a piece of Mahler's—
> I'll drink to that.

(Drinks)

And one for Mahler.

(Drinks again)

Here's to the girls who play wife—
Aren't they too much?
Keeping house but clutching a copy of *Life*
Just to keep in touch.

The ones who follow the rules,
And meet themselves at the schools,
Too busy to know that they're fools—
Aren't they a gem?
I'll drink to them.
Let's all drink to them!

And here's to the girls who just watch—
Aren't they the best?
When they get depressed, it's a bottle of Scotch
Plus a little jest.
Another chance to disapprove,
Another brilliant zinger,
Another reason not to move,
Another vodka stinger—
Aaaahh—I'll drink to that.

(Drinks)

So here's to the girls on the go—
Everybody tries.
Look into their eyes and you'll see what they know:
Everybody dies.

A toast to that invincible bunch,
The dinosaurs surviving the crunch—
Let's hear it for the ladies who lunch!
Everybody rise! Rise!
Rise! Rise! Rise! Rise! Rise! Rise!
Rise!

(The lights come back up on the nightclub)

I would like a cigarette, Larry. Remember when everyone used to smoke? How it was more—uh—festive . . .
happier or something. Now everyplace is not unlike an
operating room, for Chrissake. *(Pokes Robert)* Huh?
ROBERT: I never smoked.
JOANNE: Why?
ROBERT: I don't know. I meant to. Does that count?
JOANNE: Meant to! Meant to! Story of your life. Meant to!
Jesus, you are lifted right out of a Krafft-Ebing case his-
tory. You were always outside, looking in the window
while everybody was inside dancing at the party. Now I
insist you smoke. Your first compromise. *(She rips open
a pack of cigarettes and holds it in front of him)* Here, Rob!
Smoke!
ROBERT: No, thank you.
LARRY: Joanne, honey, c'mon—he doesn't.
ROBERT: You smoke. I'll watch.
JOANNE: Watch? Did you hear yourself? Huh? Hear what you
just said, kiddo? Watch. I am offering you a chance to . . .
ROBERT *(Interrupting)*: I don't want one.
JOANNE *(Angry, throwing the pack on the table)*: Because you're
weak . . . I hate people who are weak! *(She lights a ciga-
rette, inhales deeply, exhales)* That's the best. Better than
Prozac. Smoking may be the only thing that separates us
from the lower forms.

LARRY: You wanna split?

JOANNE: Of what?

LARRY *(To Robert)*: See, everyday Joanne tests me to see if I'll go away. Twice a year my wife here packs up to leave so I'll ask her to stay. My mother was a very difficult woman . . . and my old man left her . . . and he regretted it until the day he died. Now me, hey, I married this wildly conceited broad with no self-esteem. I got a wife who still has this hard time believing that she found a guy she daily fascinates. And, unlike my father, I'm a very happy man. She doesn't act like this when you're not around, Bobby. I hope you get to meet Joanne sometime. She's really a terrific lady. In fact, you ever decide to get married, Bobby, make sure you find someone just like Joanne.

JOANNE: Don't ever get married, Robby. Never. Why should you?

ROBERT: Oh, for company, I don't know. Like everybody else.

JOANNE: Who else?

ROBERT: Everybody that ever fell in love and got married.

JOANNE: I know both couples and they're both divorced. Oh, Larry, you interrupted me before. See what happens when you rush me. I wanted to toast my second husband.

LARRY *(Getting up)*: It's late. I'm going to the john. And when I come back we'll be leaving. The holiday is ending. Okay? *(He exits)*

ROBERT *(Calling after Larry)*: I got the check. Damn. I know he's off to pay the check.

(Joanne stares unmovingly at Robert)

Or maybe buy the place. It is a comfort to have rich friends. But I do like to pay, some of the time. Oh, well, you talked me into it! *(Pause)* You have a good third husband, Joanne. He's a good man. Anyway, thank you for the evening. I'm glad I joined you. I was really feeling low . . . really depressed. I drank, but you really put it away tonight. The last several times you and I got together, I've had shameful hangovers . . . abominable. We may be doing permanent damage—think of that? I don't know what to think of the fact that you only drink with me . . . I guess that is not unflattering. No! I hope I don't depress you! We have good times and it's a hoot, yes? Whatever you say! *(Pause)* No. I don't care for a cigarette if that is what you're trying to stare me into. I am a product of my generation and I do not smoke. My age group is a very uptight age group. Middle-age is breaking up that old gang of mine. Whew! It's very drunk out tonight. What are you looking at, Joanne? It's my charisma, huh? Well, stop looking at my charisma!

JOANNE *(Still staring)*: When are we gonna make it?

(Pause)

ROBERT: I beg your pardon?

JOANNE: When're we gonna make it?

ROBERT *(Making light of it)*: What's wrong with now?

JOANNE *(Slowly, directly)*: There's my place. It's free tomorrow after two. Larry goes to his gym, then right to the
office. Don't talk. Don't do your folksy Harold Teen
with me. You're a terribly attractive man. The kind of a
man most women want and never seem to get. I'll take
care of you.

(Pause)

ROBERT: But who will I take care of?

JOANNE: Well, did you hear yourself? Did you hear what you just said, kiddo?

ROBERT: I didn't mean that.

JOANNE: Oh, I just heard a door open that's been stuck a long time.

ROBERT: Like I haven't looked at all that? At marriages and all that? And what do you get for it? What do you get?

LARRY *(Re-enters)*: Well, the check is paid and . . . *(Looks at the emotional Robert)* What's wrong?

ROBERT: I've looked at all that—marriages and all that—and what do you get for it? What do you get? *(He leaves the table)*

LARRY: What happened?

JOANNE: I just did someone a big favor. C'mon, Larry, let's us go home.

(Joanne and Larry exit. Underscoring: "Bobby Baby" music)

ROBERT *(To himself)*: What do you get?!

JENNY:

Bobby . . .

PETER:

Bobby . . .

AMY:

Bobby baby . . .

PAUL:

Bobby bubi . . .

HARRY:

Robby . . .

SARAH:

Robert darling . . .

DAVID:

Bobby, we've been trying to call you.

JENNY:

Bobby . . .

LARRY:

Bobby . . .

AMY:

Bobby baby . . .

PAUL:

Bobby bubi . . .

SARAH:

Angel, I've got something to tell you.

HARRY:

Bob . . .

LARRY:

Rob-o . . .

JOANNE:

Bobby, love . . .

SUSAN:

Bobby, honey . . .

AMY & PAUL:
> Bobby, we've been trying to reach you
> All day.

LARRY:
> Bobby . . .

HARRY:
> Bobby . . .

PETER:
> Bobby baby . . .

SARAH:
> Angel . . .

JOANNE:
> Darling . . .

DAVID & JENNY:
> The kids were asking, Bobby . . .

HARRY:
> Bobby . . .

SUSAN:
> Robert . . .

JOANNE:
> Robby . . .

PETER:
> Bob-o . . .

LARRY & JOANNE:
>Bobby, there was something we wanted to say.

SARAH & HARRY:
>Bobby . . .

PAUL:
>Bobby bubi . . .

AMY:
>Sweetheart . . .

SUSAN:
>Sugar . . .

DAVID & JENNY:
>Your line was busy.

ALL BUT ROBERT:
>Bobby . . .

ROBERT:
>Stop!
>What do you get?
>
>Someone to hold you too close,
>Someone to hurt you too deep,
>Someone to sit in your chair,
>To ruin your sleep . . .

PAUL: That's true, but there's more than that.

SARAH: Is that all you think there is to it?

HARRY: You've got so many reasons for not being with someone, but Robert, you haven't got one good reason for
being alone.

LARRY: Come on. You're on to something, Bobby. You're on to something.

ROBERT:

> Someone to need you too much,
> Someone to know you too well,
> Someone to pull you up short
> And put you through hell . . .

JOANNE: You're not a kid anymore, Robert. I don't think you'll ever be a kid again, kiddo.

PETER: Hey, buddy. Don't be afraid it won't be perfect . . . the only thing to be afraid of really is that it won't *be*!

JENNY: Don't stop now! Keep going!

ROBERT:

> Someone you have to let in.
> Someone whose feelings you spare,
> Someone who, like it or not, will want you to share
> A little a lot . . .

SUSAN: And what does all that mean!

LARRY: Robert, how do you know so much about it when you've never been there?

HARRY: It's all much better living it than looking at it, Robert.

PETER: Add 'em up, Bobby. Add 'em up.

ROBERT:

> Someone to crowd you with love,
> Someone to force you to care,
> Someone to make you come through,
> Who'll always be there, as frightened as you,
> Of being alive,
> Being alive, being alive, being alive.

AMY: Blow out your candles, Robert, and make a wish. *Want*
something, Robert! Want *something*!

ROBERT:

    Somebody hold me too close,
    Somebody hurt me too deep,
    Somebody sit in my chair
    And ruin my sleep and make me aware
    Of being alive, being alive.

    Somebody need me too much,
    Somebody know me too well,
    Somebody pull me up short
    And put me through hell and give me support
    For being alive.
    Make me alive,
    Make me alive.

    Make me confused,
    Mock me with praise,
    Let me be used,
    Vary my days.
    But alone is alone, not alive.

    Somebody crowd me with love,
    Somebody force me to care,
    Somebody let me come through,
    I'll always be there
    As frightened as you,
    To help us survive
    Being alive, being alive, being alive.

(Lights come up on Scene Five)

Scene Five

Robert's apartment. The birthday party again.

COUPLES:

> Bobby, Bobby . . .
> Ba ba ba ba ba ba ba ba
> Bobby, Bobby . . .
> Ba ba ba ba ba ba ba ba
> Bobby . . .

(We hear footsteps in the distance growing louder. The lights are turned down; a key is heard in a lock, but it is another door in the building that opens and closes. Pause)

LARRY: Must have been the apartment across the hall.

(Pause)

HARRY: This is the craziest thing . . . huh?

AMY: Do you think something's wrong?

PAUL: No. I think something's right.

AMY: So do I.

PETER: Well, I've called every joint in town.

SUSAN: It *has* been over two hours now. Maybe he forgot.

SARAH: How can anyone forget a surprise birthday?

JOANNE: Or . . . maybe the surprise is on us. I think I got the message. C'mon, Larry, let's go home.

LARRY: Yeah. I think we should.

PAUL: Yes, I think we can go now.

SARAH: Maybe we should leave him a note.

HARRY: Maybe we should leave him alone.

SUSAN: I'll call him tomorrow.
PETER: Don't.
SUSAN: I won't.
JENNY: David?
DAVID: What?
JENNY: Nothing.
JOANNE: Okay. All together, everybody.
ALL: Happy birthday, Robert.

> *(They exit the apartment, leaving it empty.*
> *From out of the shadows in the rear of the stage steps*
> *Robert. Unbeknownst to us, he has been observing the action.*
> *He now sits on the sofa and takes a moment. Then he smiles,*
> *leans forward and blows out the candles)*

CURTAIN